A Note About Safety

Although the building methods shown in *My First Project* are considered safe practice in the woodworking industry, the responsibility for working safely ultimately rests on your shoulders. As a result, the publisher of this book (Grassland Publishing and EZwoodshop.com) assumes no responsibility for damages, injuries suffered, or losses incurred as a result of following the information that is presented in this book.

Remember that power tools can be especially dangerous. Spend time with your owner's manual to learn how a tool operates, the safety features included with that tool, and any other information the tool manufacturer thinks you should know before using that tool. This book is intended to supplement the owner's manual, not replace it.

Also, it's your responsibility to protect yourself against the potential health hazards of working with wood. That means using protective eye wear (safety glasses, goggles), ear protection (plugs, earmuffs), and dust control products (respiratory masks and dust filters). Also, if fatigue, stress, or other physical problems are affecting your best judgment, stop working and return to the shop on another day.

Don't let impatience and carelessness ruin the fun!

Want to Learn More?

If you like what you see in *My First Project,* visit my website for more how-to guides, building techniques, and wood project ideas.

www.ezwoodshop.com

■EZ Wood Tools
■EZ Wood Project Books
■EZ Wood Project Plans

My First Project
Contents

EZ Cutting Station 3
Cutting Station Anatomy 4
Getting Started: Tools & Materials...................5
EZ Cutlist 8
Pilot Hole Diagram..12
Start Building: Cutting Station Base 13
Next Steps: Build the Panel Cutter 16

EZ Workbench 23
Workbench Anatomy 24
Getting Started: Tools & Materials...................25
Design Your Workbench......................................26
EZ Cutlist 31
Pilot Hole Diagram..34
Start Building..35
Next Steps: Add a Lower Shelf 40
Next Steps: Build a Side Table 41
2x4 Joinery 42

EZ Bookcase 45
Bookcase Anatomy 46
Getting Started: Tools & Materials...................47
Design Your Bookcase..48
EZ Cutlist 52
Pilot Hole Diagram..55
Start Building..56
Next Steps: Add Trim...65
Next Steps: Add Center Dividers.......................66
Next Steps: Add a Finish 67
Next Steps: How to Seal Knots 70

 BOOK CUTOUTS

The pages below are designed to be cut out from this book for use in the shop.

✂ EZ Pilot Hole Guides: Cutting Station 73
✂ EZ Pilot Hole Guides: Workbench 79
✂ EZ Pilot Hole Guides: Bookcase 85

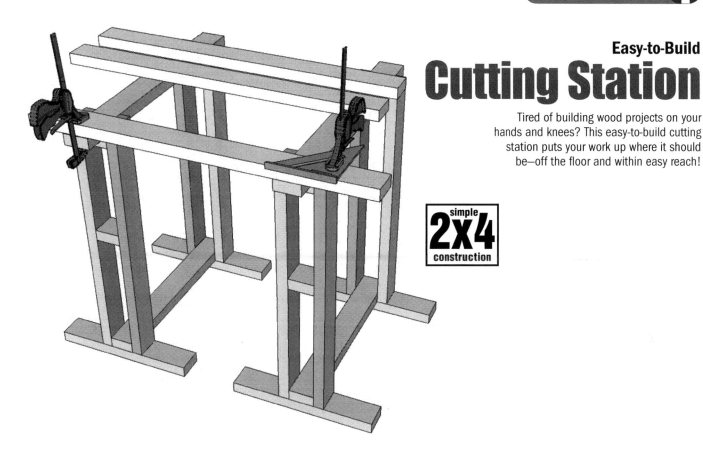

Easy-to-Build
Cutting Station

Tired of building wood projects on your hands and knees? This easy-to-build cutting station puts your work up where it should be—off the floor and within easy reach!

simple 2X4 construction

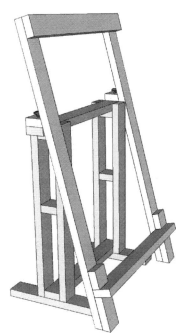

■ **Cut Plywood Panels.** The optional EZ Panel Cutter makes working with plywood a snap. Features knock-down hardware for easy removal and storage.

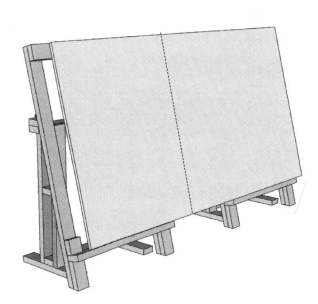

■ **Build a Pair!** Building two EZ Cutting Stations gives you a complete workstation that can handle full-size sheets of plywood.

Cutting Station: Anatomy

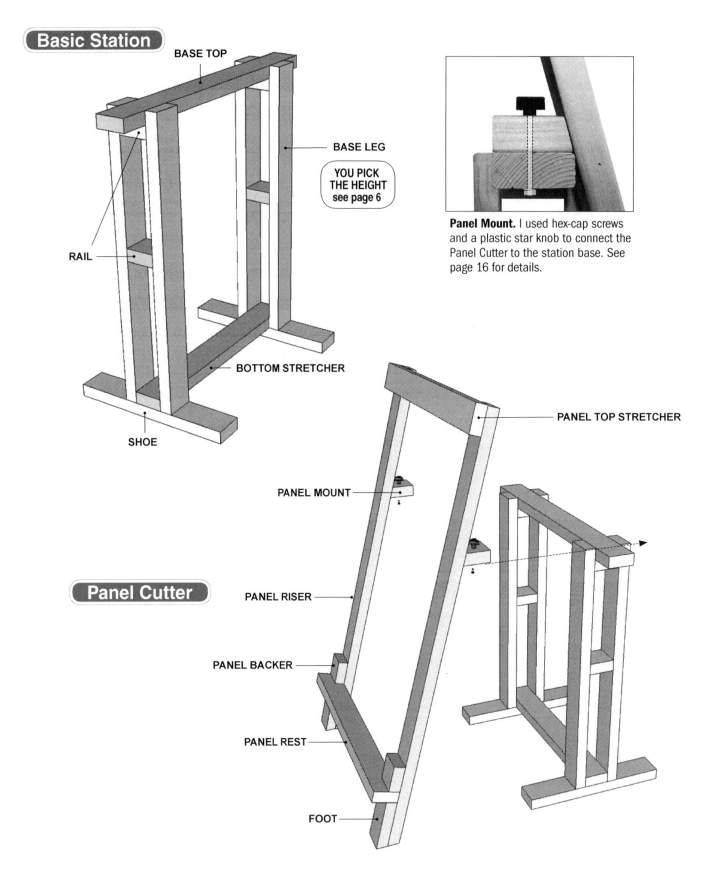

Basic Station

BASE TOP

BASE LEG

YOU PICK
THE HEIGHT
see page 6

RAIL

BOTTOM STRETCHER

SHOE

Panel Mount. I used hex-cap screws and a plastic star knob to connect the Panel Cutter to the station base. See page 16 for details.

PANEL TOP STRETCHER

PANEL MOUNT

Panel Cutter

PANEL RISER

PANEL BACKER

PANEL REST

FOOT

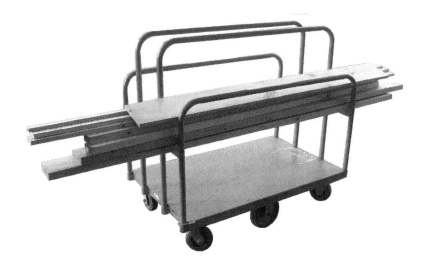

Getting Started

The EZ Cutting Station is the perfect starting point for learning the basic skills construction skills you'll need for other projects. It's also a crucial piece of shop furniture that will make an easy job of cutting and assembling the different parts of a project. As you can see below, the tools and materials needed for this project are simple and inexpensive. In fact, I'm guessing you might already have a few of the items in your shop or garage. If not, you can easily find them at your local home improvement store.

What's Next?

On the following pages, I'll take you step by step through the process of choosing the best height for your cutting station, determining what length to cut the boards, and assembling the pieces. Let's get started!

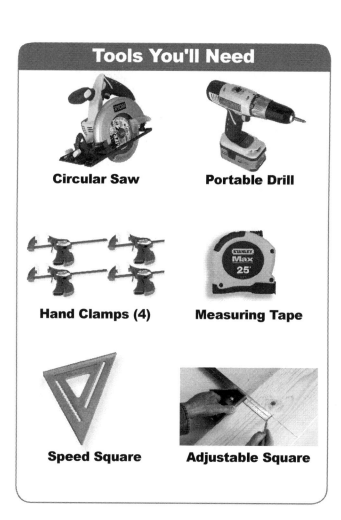

Tools You'll Need

Circular Saw

Portable Drill

Hand Clamps (4)

Measuring Tape

Speed Square

Adjustable Square

Lumber & Hardware

2x4 Boards
(see page 8)

#6 - #8 - #10 - #12
Countersink Bit

Drill Bit Set

1 BOX
2½" Drywall Screw

¼" Lock Washer

¼" x 3½" Hex Cap Screw

¼"–20 Star Knob

Your Design | Choose Height

A good rule of thumb to follow for setting the height of any type of workstation is to make the top even with the bottom edge of your shirt cuff. For example, someone 5'-10" inches tall would find a 36" top surface to be just about right.

Although the shirt-cuff rule provides a good starting point, some types of work are better suited for different bench heights. For example, if you want to use the cutting station for sanding, planing, or carving, a shorter height might make more sense (see examples below). For assembly and repair work, I prefer something a little taller. Workstation height is important because standing for long periods at a table that is too low—or too high—can cause muscle fatigue and back strain.

My Choice for Station Height: _____

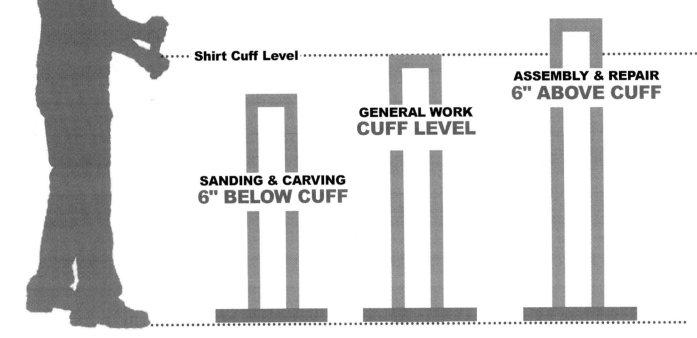

Shirt Cuff Level

ASSEMBLY & REPAIR
6" ABOVE CUFF

GENERAL WORK
CUFF LEVEL

SANDING & CARVING
6" BELOW CUFF

EZ TIPS

Do You Have a Level Shop?

If you plan to build other workstations in your shop (workbench and side table), consider making them *all the same height*. This will give you a nice support system for working with long boards and extra-large project pieces.

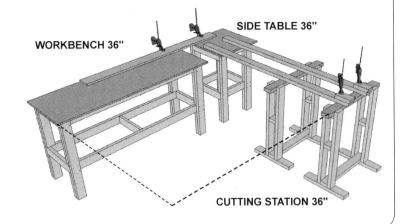

WORKBENCH 36"

SIDE TABLE 36"

CUTTING STATION 36"

Make a Cutlist
Leg Length

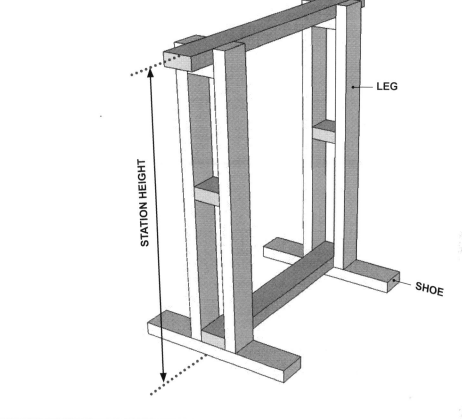

LEG

STATION HEIGHT

SHOE

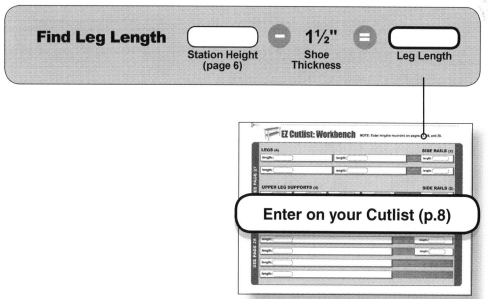

Find Leg Length ☐ − **1½"** = ☐

Station Height
(page 6)

Shoe
Thickness

Leg Length

Enter on your Cutlist (p.8)

2x4 simple construction

Cut all pieces from 2x4 dimensional lumber.

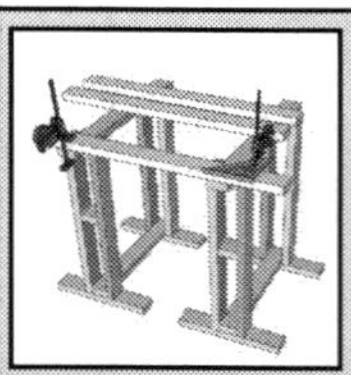

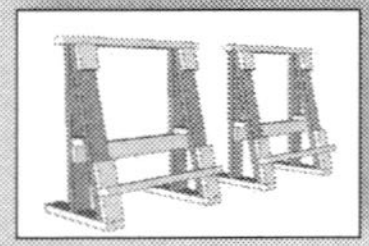

Building a Pair?
The cutlist below is for **ONE** cutting station **ONLY**.
If you are building a pair, simply double the quantity.

Cutting Station

| Top: | 34 ¾" |

| Bottom Stretcher: | 28" |

| Leg: | (your choice: page 7) | Shoe: | 20" |

| Leg: | (your choice: page 7) | Shoe: | 20" |

| Leg: | (your choice: page 7) |

| Leg: | (your choice: page 7) |

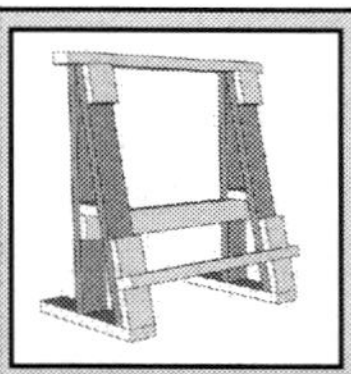

RAILS 3½" each

Panel Cutter (optional)

Note: ///// Symbol indicates bevel - see page 6

| PANEL TOP STRETCHER 34 ¾" |

| PANEL REST 34 ¾" |

PANEL MOUNT: 3½"

PANEL FOOT: 6"

PANEL BACKER: 3½"

| PANEL RISER 58" |

| PANEL RISER 58" |

Cut Boards to Size

Whenever I build a project that has a lot of different pieces, I like to first cut the boards down to the sizes I need. This not only keeps my project better organized, but also makes it easier keep like pieces *exactly the same length*—which is often more important than the actual length itself.

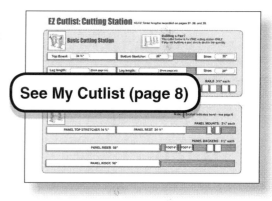

See My Cutlist (page 8)

On page 8 you'll find a diagram showing all the pieces that make up the cutting station, along with the length needed for each piece. You'll need to buy six 2x4 boards (8 ft.) to complete one cutting station, or 12 boards to make a matching pair. However, I recommend buying an extra board or two in case you make a cutting mistake (it happens to all of us!).

Note that a few pieces in the panel support assembly require a *bevel cut at one end*. See page 10 for more about cutting bevels with your circular saw.

Cutting Tips & Tricks

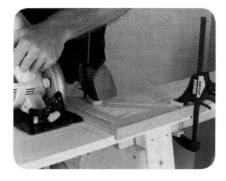

Speed Square
A plastic rafter square (speed square) makes a nice cutting guide for your circular saw. I like to clamp the square and keep both hands on the saw.

Safe Stop
Always let the blade come to a complete stop before moving the saw away (a blade will continue spinning for several seconds after it stops).

Gang Up Boards
The fewer cuts you make, the fewer chances for mistakes. That's why I like to "gang up" same-size project pieces and cut them all in one swoop.

Cutting Bevels

The EZ Panel Cutter (optional) leans against the cutting station at an angle—just enough to keep plywood from falling forward. This means some of the boards will need to be cut with a bevel at one end. Look for the bevel setting toward the front of your saw (see below) and lock in place at 15 degrees.

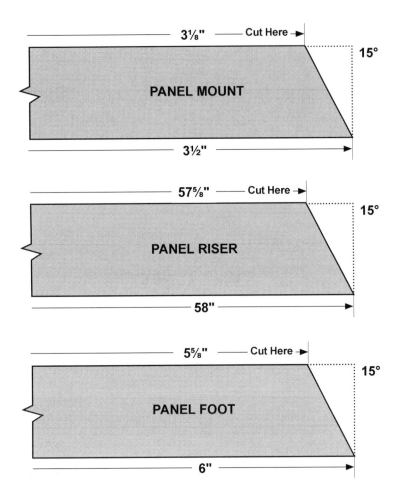

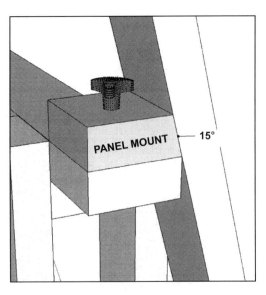

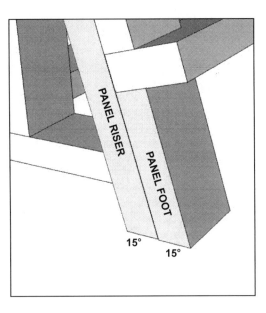

Bevel Tips & Tricks

The tricky part about cutting a bevel is figuring out where to draw the cut line. Keep in mind that a 15 degree bevel will make one side of your board ⅜" shorter than the other. For example, to create a 58" board with a bevel at one end (see panel riser above), draw your cut line at 57 ⅝".

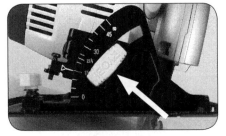

Look for the bevel knob located at the front of your circular saw.

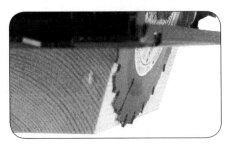

When cutting bevels in 2x4s, extend the blade depth as far as it will go.

Drill Pilot Holes

See Pilot Hole Guides (page 73)

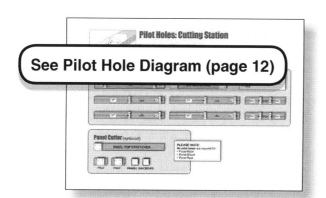

See Pilot Hole Diagram (page 12)

Drilling pilot holes can be a time-consuming job if you leave this task for each stage of construction. I've found that it's much easier to mark and drill pilot holes in *advance,* just after cutting all your project pieces to size.

Pre-drilling pilot holes will definitely speed up the assembly process later on, but the big advantage here is that it's much easier to measure and mark pilot hole locations when boards are laid out on a flat surface within easy reach.

On page 12 you'll find a diagram showing where to drill pilot holes on each project piece. Use the EZ Pilot Hole Guides (page 73) to help you align the location of the holes.

EZ Pilot Hole Guides

The *location* of the pilot hole is just as important as the hole itself. If it's not in the right place, you can easily ruin a project by splitting the fragile edges of the boards you're trying to join.

That's why I've included a set of pilot hole guides (page 73) to make the task easy.
You can cut the templates directly out of this book, and then line them up along the end of each board.
I like to use an ice pick or a woodworker's awl to mark the locations. This will also create a nice starter hole for inserting your drill bit.

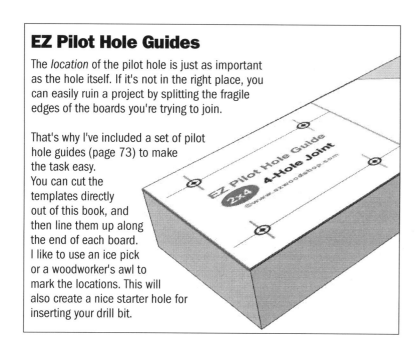

Use Countersink Bit

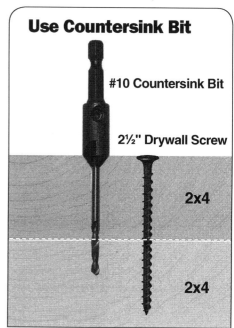

#10 Countersink Bit

2½" Drywall Screw

2x4

2x4

Pilot Hole Diagram: EZ Cutting Station

Cut the templates directly out of this book, and then line them up along the end of each board. I like to use an ice pick or a woodworker's awl to mark the locations. This will also create a nice starter hole for inserting your drill bit.

Basic Cutting Station

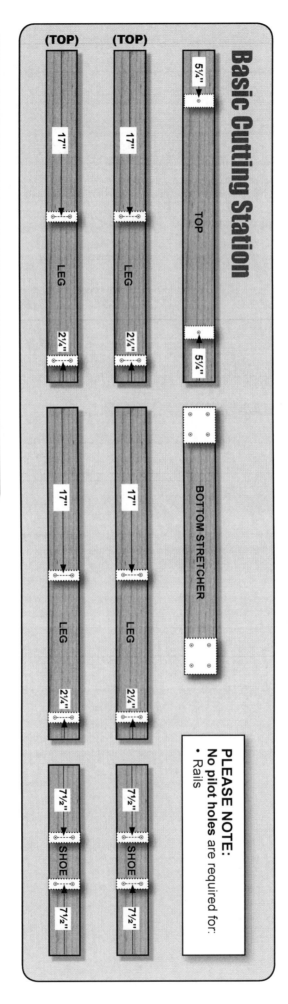

(TOP) **(TOP)**

5¼" TOP 5¼"

17" 17" LEG LEG 2¼" 2¼"

BOTTOM STRETCHER

17" 17" LEG LEG 2¼" 2¼"

7½" 7½" SHOE SHOE 7½" 7½"

PLEASE NOTE:
No pilot holes are required for:
• Rails

Panel Cutter (optional)

PANEL TOP STRETCHER

FOOT
FOOT
PANEL BACKERS
• center on board

PLEASE NOTE:
No pilot holes are required for:
• Panel Riser
• Panel Mount
• Panel Rest

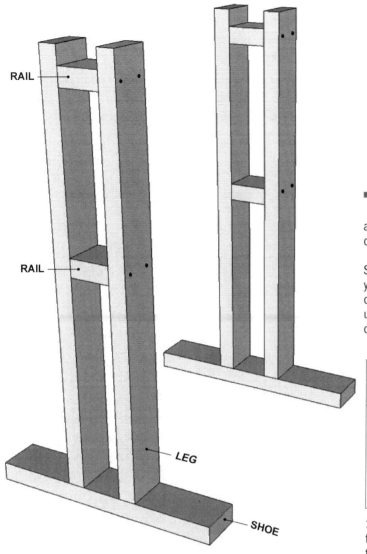

RAIL

RAIL

LEG

SHOE

Start Building! The Legs 1

The best way to guarantee a wobble-free cutting station is to make sure all joints are straight and square. The leg assembly, more than any other component of this project, is crucial to the overall stability of the cutting station.

Start by finding a table or shelf somewhere in the house that you can borrow—just long enough to get these first few joints completed. Make sure it has a sharp, square corner. Then line up all the pieces of the leg assembly along the edge using a carpenter's square and few hand clamps (see below).

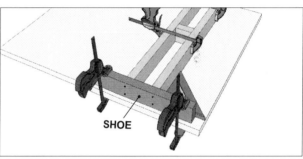

SHOE

1. Attach Shoe. I like to start at the shoe, driving screws in from the bottom and up into the legs. First make sure everything the entire assembly is straight, square, and clamped in place.

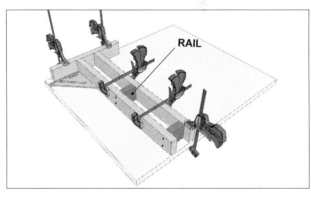

RAIL

2. Attach Rails. With the clamps still in place, move on to the legs and attach the rails. If you can't get the screws go in completely, try drilling a deeper pilot hole into the rail.

Glue?

Although it's possible to build a strong cutting station without, glue will add additional strength. Apply a generous amount to *one side* of the joint only.

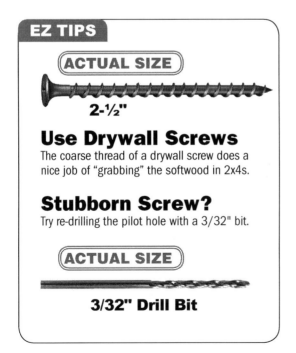

EZ TIPS

ACTUAL SIZE

2-½"

Use Drywall Screws
The coarse thread of a drywall screw does a nice job of "grabbing" the softwood in 2x4s.

Stubborn Screw?
Try re-drilling the pilot hole with a 3/32" bit.

ACTUAL SIZE

3/32" Drill Bit

2 Add Bottom Stretcher

It's Coming Together!

This step in the project gives you a sneak peak at how the finished project will look! Don't lose your concentration, though. This is another critical step where everything needs to be aligned with as much accuracy as possible. Use the same square-edged table you used in step 1, and line up the shoe and bottom stretcher as shown in the illustration below. As always, use plenty of clamps to hold everything secure while you drive the screws.

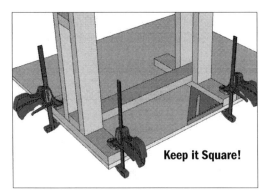

Keep it Square!

Start by finding a smooth and flat surface somewhere in the house that you can borrow—just long enough to get these first few joints completed.

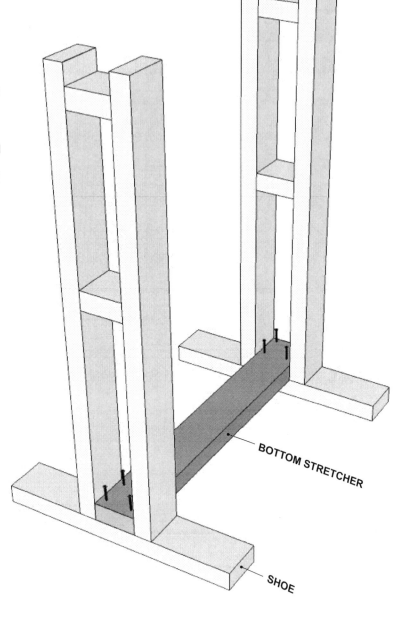

BOTTOM STRETCHER

SHOE

EZ TIPS

ACTUAL SIZE

2-½"

Use Drywall Screws

The coarse thread of a drywall screw does a nice job of "grabbing" the softwood in 2x4s.

Stubborn Screw?

Try re-drilling the pilot hole with a 3/32" bit.

ACTUAL SIZE

3/32" Drill Bit

Glue?

Although it's possible to build a strong cutting station without, glue will add additional strength. Apply a generous amount to *one side* of the joint only.

TOP

Attach Top 3

All that's left now is to slip the top into place and drive two screws at each end. Don't worry if the fit is a little snug—that only means you did a great job measuring and cutting! A couple taps with a scrap board (or a rubber mallet) should push the top piece into position.

Remember to allow approximately 3½" overhang at each end. You'll need this extra space for attaching clamps when cutting boards, and also for attaching the optional panel cutting assembly.

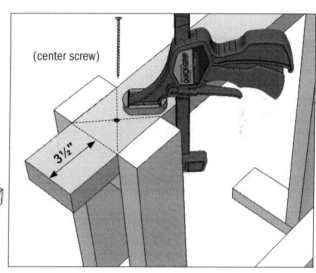

(center screw)

3½"

Allow 3½" overhang at each end.

EZ TIPS

ACTUAL SIZE

2-1/2"

Use Drywall Screws

The coarse thread of a drywall screw does a nice job of "grabbing" the softwood in 2x4s.

Stubborn Screw?

Try re-drilling the pilot hole with a 3/32" bit.

ACTUAL SIZE

3/32" Drill Bit

Glue?

Although it's possible to build a strong cutting station without, glue will add additional strength. Apply a generous amount to *one side* of the joint only.

NEXT STEPS
Panel Cutter

Plywood is one of my favorite materials for building simple wood projects. Unfortunately, the large panels (4' x 8') can be difficult to work with, especially in a small workshop. That's why plywood usually ends up on the floor, where you have to get down on your hands and knees to measure, mark, and cut the panel. Not very fun.

This simple accessory takes plywood off the floor—and puts it up within easy reach. It also provides a nice place to store plywood for an upcoming project—away from concrete floors and walls (to avoid moisture damage) and conveniently tucked away in a corner.

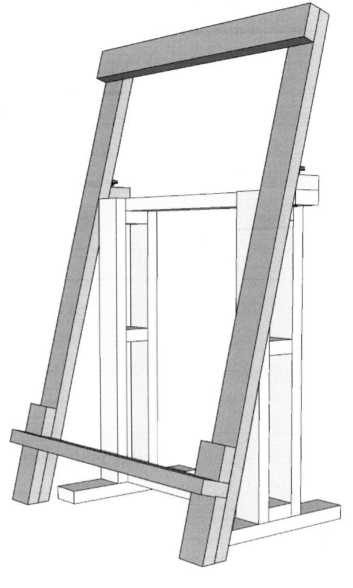

The best way to take full advantage of the EZ Panel Cutter is to *build a pair* of cutting stations (see above). This arrangement lets you support a full sheet of 4x8 plywood across both stations.

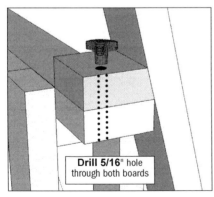

Drill 5/16" hole through both boards

See page 19 to read more about installing this hardware.

EZ Knock-Down Hardware!

Not all wood projects call for plywood, so I designed the EZ Panel Cutter to be easily removed from the cutting station when not in use. An inexpensive pair of star knobs and bolts makes a nice choice for easy-to-remove hardware.

You'll need to drill a fairly large hole through both the panel mount and the base top (5/16") to allow the bolt to slip through both boards. A simple lock washer will hold everything in place while you tighten down the star knob.

Star knobs are easy to find at your local hardware store or home center.

Assemble Panel Risers 1

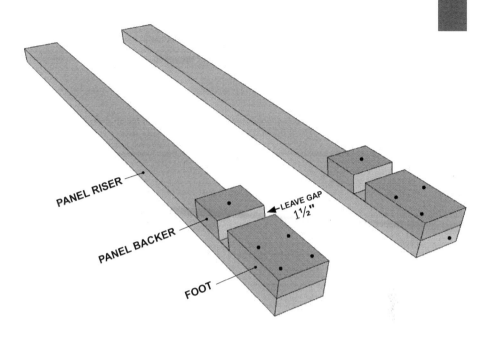

PANEL RISER

PANEL BACKER

LEAVE GAP 1½"

FOOT

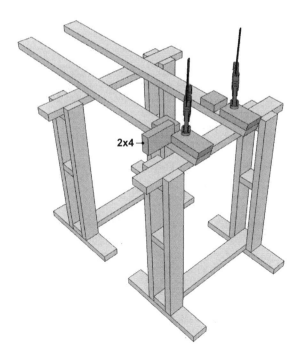

2x4

Leave a Gap

As you'll discover on the next page, the gap I'm showing here between the *panel foot* and the *panel backer* (see above) should be just wide enough to fit the thickness of the *panel rest* (1½"). No need to measure here—just use a scrap piece of 2x4 (or the panel rest itself) as a guide for setting the correct gap.

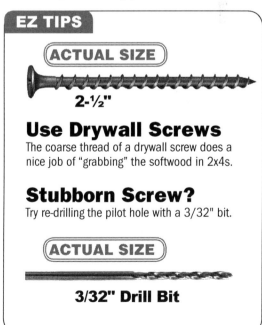

EZ TIPS

ACTUAL SIZE

2-½"

Use Drywall Screws
The coarse thread of a drywall screw does a nice job of "grabbing" the softwood in 2x4s.

Stubborn Screw?
Try re-drilling the pilot hole with a 3/32" bit.

ACTUAL SIZE

3/32" Drill Bit

Glue?
Although it's possible to build a strong cutting station without, glue will add additional strength. Apply a generous amount to *one side* of the joint only.

2 Add Top Stretcher & Panel Rest

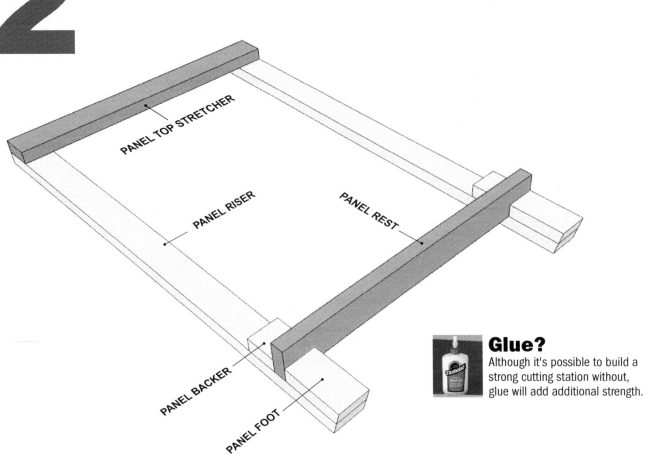

PANEL TOP STRETCHER

PANEL RISER

PANEL REST

PANEL BACKER

PANEL FOOT

Glue?
Although it's possible to build a strong cutting station without, glue will add additional strength.

EZ TIPS

ACTUAL SIZE

2-½"

Use Drywall Screws
The coarse thread of a drywall screw does a nice job of "grabbing" the softwood in 2x4s.

Stubborn Screw?
Try re-drilling the pilot hole with a 3/32" bit.

ACTUAL SIZE

3/32" Drill Bit

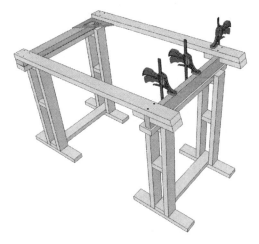

Drive Screws from Back
The easiest way to complete this part of the panel cutter is to drive the screws in from the back (see drawing at left). First be sure that the assembly is straight and square (check the corners with a carpenter's square) and position the clamps as close to the pilot holes as possible.

Panel Mounts 3

Most of the work I do at my cutting station consists of chopping off the ends of 2x4s and assembling project pieces—not cutting plywood. That's why I designed the panel cutter to be easily removed when not in use. A "star knob" with a hex-cap screw makes the perfect fastener for attaching—and removing—the panel cutter assembly from the cutting station base. Star knobs, screws, and lock washers can be found at your local hardware store.

As you can see in the photo at left, I've drilled a large hole through the panel mount and the base top, which provides just enough room for the bolt to slip through both boards. You'll need a 5/16" drill bit to make the hole, which is a fairly common size included in most drill bit sets. The lock washer holds the bolt steady while you turn the star knob.

Here's What You'll Need

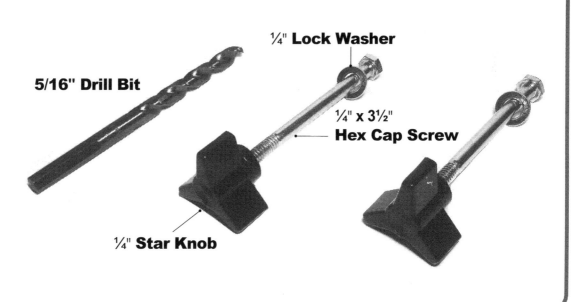

5/16" Drill Bit

¼" **Lock Washer**

¼" x 3½"
Hex Cap Screw

¼" **Star Knob**

4 Attach Panel Mounts

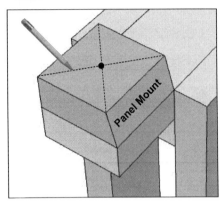

1. Find Center

Position panel mounts over base top. Draw diagonal lines from each corner to find center.

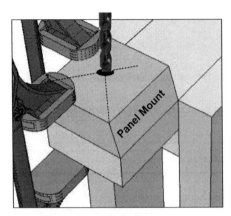

2. Clamp & Drill

Drill a 5/16" hole through both the panel mount and the base top. Be sure to use clamps!

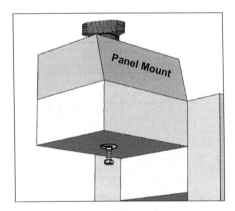

3. Attach Hardware

Insert bolt (with lock washer) from below, and then attach star knob on top. Tighten down.

4. Line Up Panel Risers

Lean panel cutter assembly against the cutting station base. Make beveled feet flush with floor.

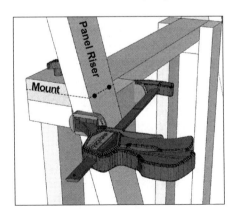

5. Mark Pilot Holes

Clamp panel riser to the cutting station base. Mark pilot hole locations (along center line).

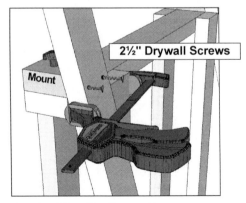

6. Drill/Drive Screws

Drill pilot holes and then drive screws through panel riser and into panel mount.

Congratulations!

Your Project is Complete!

Hopefully this journey has taught you some valuable skills that you can use to build more wood projects in the future. Now that you have a rock-solid cutting station ready to go, new projects will be much easier to complete. Now it's time to put this workstation to work!

What's Next?

Second on my list for must-have items in a home workshop is a workbench. My EZ Workbench Plan gives you easy-to-follow instructions for both designing and building a workbench to fit your space, your style.

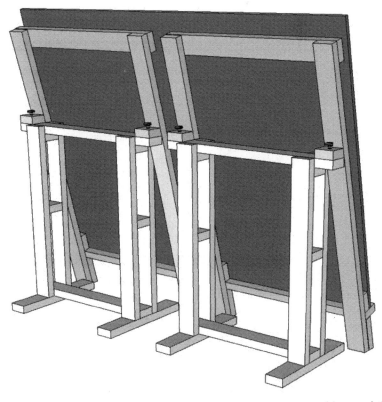

EZ Cutting Station

Cutting Station & Panel Cutter

my first project 2

Design Your Own

simple 2x4 construction **Workbench**

Build a Matching Side Table!

WorkBench Anatomy

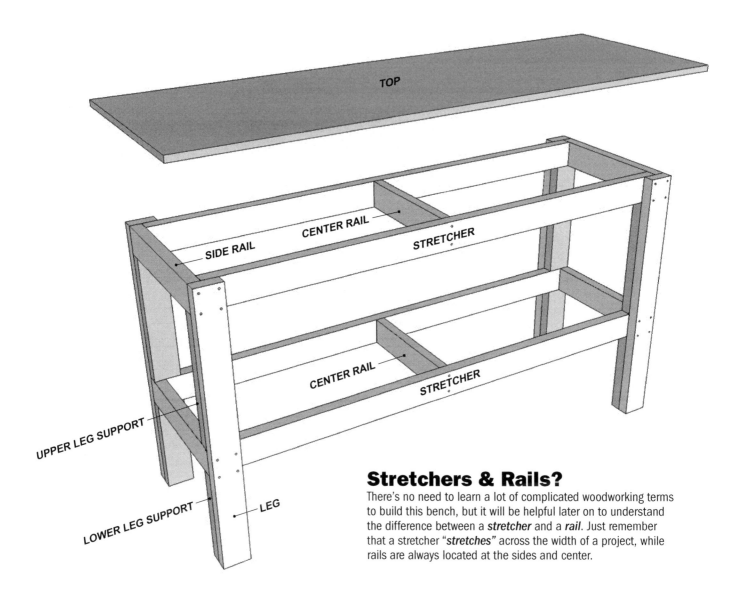

TOP

CENTER RAIL

SIDE RAIL

STRETCHER

CENTER RAIL

STRETCHER

UPPER LEG SUPPORT

LOWER LEG SUPPORT

LEG

Stretchers & Rails?

There's no need to learn a lot of complicated woodworking terms to build this bench, but it will be helpful later on to understand the difference between a *stretcher* and a *rail*. Just remember that a stretcher "*stretches*" across the width of a project, while rails are always located at the sides and center.

Getting Started

Building a workbench from scratch might seem a little intimidating at first, especially to those who are just getting started in the craft. Not to fear—this project plan is especially designed for DIY newbies!

As you can see below, the tools and materials needed for this project are simple and inexpensive. In fact, I'm guessing you might already have a few of the items in your shop or garage. If not, you can easily find them at your local home improvement store.

What's Next?

On the following pages, I'll take you step by step through the process of choosing the best size for your workbench, cutting the boards to length, and assembling the pieces. Let's get started!

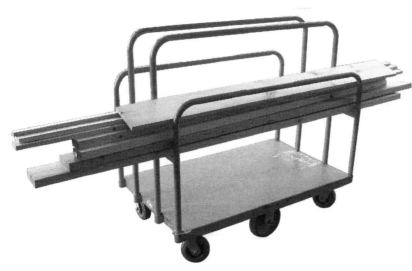

Tools You'll Need

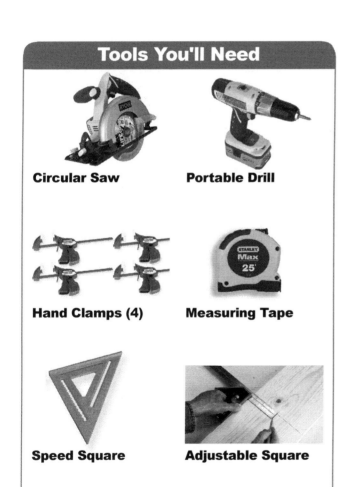

Circular Saw   **Portable Drill**

Hand Clamps (4)   **Measuring Tape**

Speed Square   **Adjustable Square**

Lumber & Hardware

2x4 Boards   **Plywood**

Countersink Bit Set
#6 - #8 - #10 - #12   **Drill Bit Set**

1 BOX — 2½" **Drywall Screws**

1 BOX — 1¼" **Drywall Screws**   **Wood Glue**

Your Design Choose Workbench Top

The workbench tops shown here are suggestions only. You can choose whatever bench size you like with this plan! It's always a good idea to first choose a location for the bench (a basement wall, a corner of the garage, etc.) and then design your bench to fit that space.

My Choice for Workbench Top: _____ **X** _____
WIDTH   DEPTH

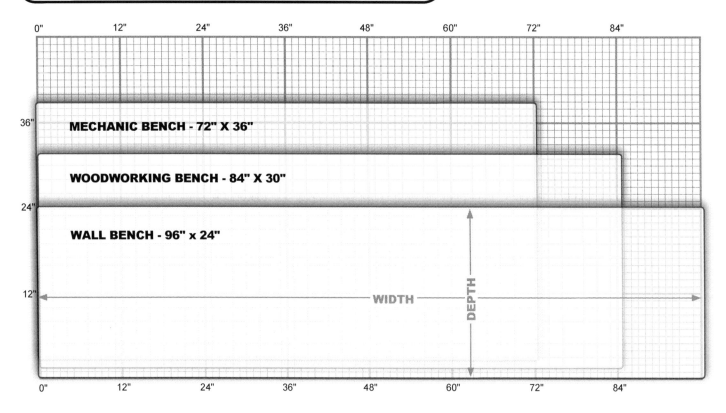

Want a Different Size?

The workbench tops shown here are *suggestions only.* Choose whatever bench size you like!

Choose Workbench Height

A good rule of thumb to follow for setting the height of a workbench is to make the top even with the bottom edge of your shirt cuff. For example, someone 5'-10" inches tall would find a 36" bench height to be just about right.

Although the shirt-cuff rule provides a good starting point, some types of work are better suited for different bench heights. For example, if you want to use the bench for sanding, planing, or carving, a shorter bench might make more sense (see examples below). For assembly and repair work, I prefer a taller bench. Bench height is important because standing at a workstation that is too low—or too high—can cause muscle fatigue and back strain.

My Choice for Workbench Height: _____

Shirt Cuff Level ....

SANDING/PLANING
6" BELOW CUFF

GENERAL WORK
CUFF LEVEL

ASSEMBLY/REPAIR
6" ABOVE CUFF

EZ TIPS

Do You Have a Level Shop?

If you plan to build other workstations in your shop (side table and cutting station), consider making them *all the same height*. This will give you a nice support system for working with long boards and extra-large project pieces.

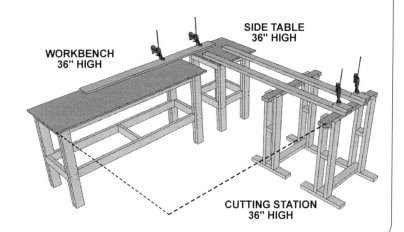

WORKBENCH
36" HIGH

SIDE TABLE
36" HIGH

CUTTING STATION
36" HIGH

Make Your Cutlist
Find Leg Length

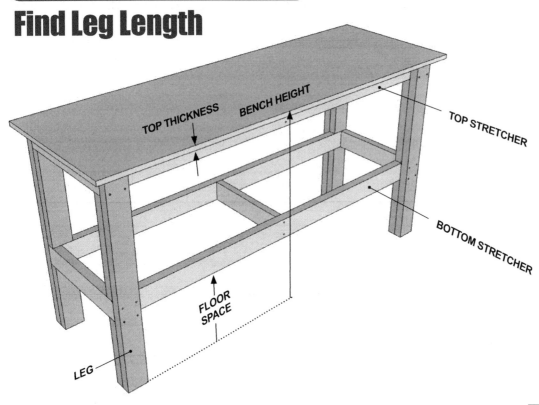

Find Length for Legs

Bench Height (page 27)	⊖	Top Thickness	⊜	Leg Length

Find Length for Upper Leg Supports

Leg Length (from above)	⊖	3½" Top Stretcher	⊖	3½" Bottom Stretcher	⊖	Floor Space	⊜	Upper Leg Support

Find Length for Lower Leg Supports

Floor Space (see drawing)	⊜	Lower Leg Support

Enter on Cutlist (p.31)

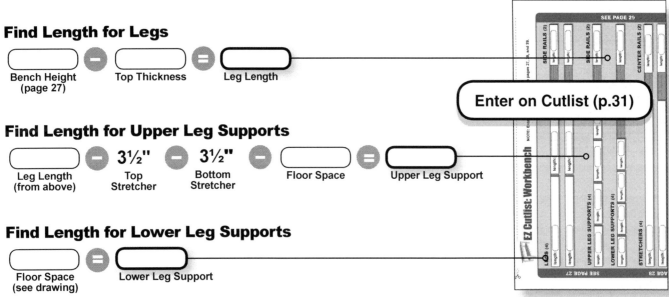

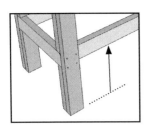

How Much Floor Space?

It's your decision how much space to allow between the floor and the bottom shelf area. I like to leave at least enough space to get a broom under for cleaning.

Make Your Cutlist
Find Stretcher Length

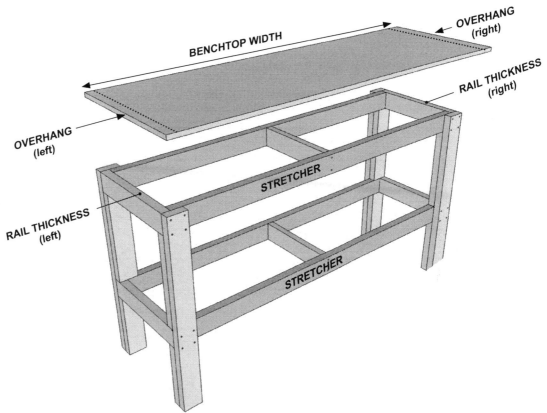

Find Length for Stretchers

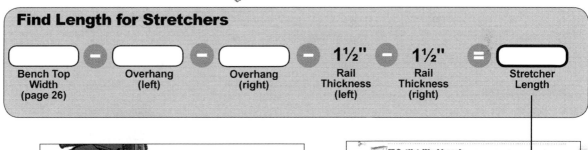

| Bench Top Width (page 26) | − | Overhang (left) | − | Overhang (right) | − | 1½" Rail Thickness (left) | − | 1½" Rail Thickness (right) | = | Stretcher Length |

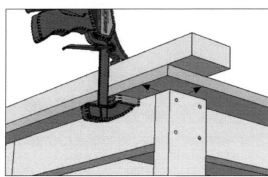

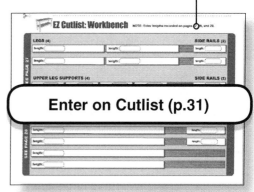

Enter on Cutlist (p.31)

How Much Overhang?

An overhang at the edge of your bench comes in handy for clamping project pieces and accessories. I built my bench with a 3" overhang on all sides.

Make Your Cutlist
Find Rail Length

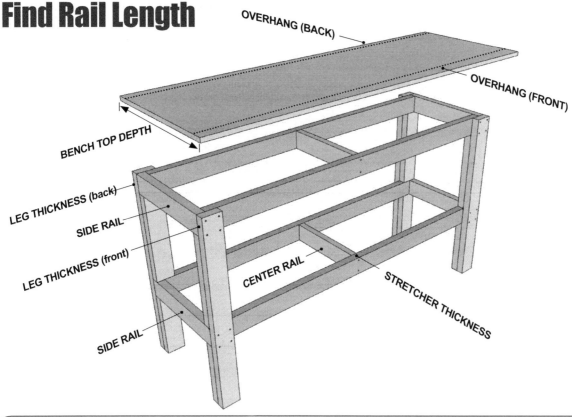

OVERHANG (BACK)

OVERHANG (FRONT)

BENCH TOP DEPTH

LEG THICKNESS (back)

SIDE RAIL

LEG THICKNESS (front)

SIDE RAIL

CENTER RAIL

STRETCHER THICKNESS

Find Length for Side Rails

| Bench Top Depth (page 26) | − | Overhang (front) | − | Overhang (back) | − | 1½" Leg Thickness (front) | − | 1½" Leg Thickness (back) | = | Side Rail Length |

Find Length for Center Rails

| Side Rail Length (see above) | − | 1½" Stretcher Thickness (front) | − | 1½" Stretcher Thickness (back) | = | Center Rail Length |

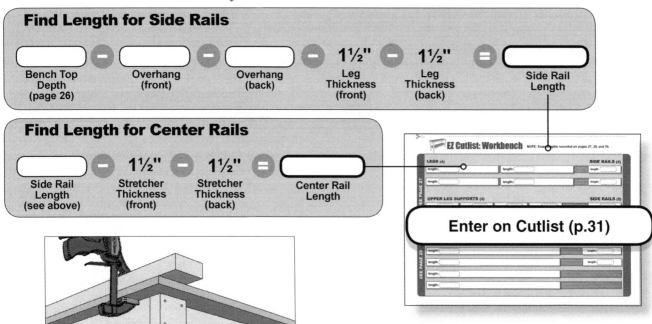

Enter on Cutlist (p.31)

EZ Cutlist: Workbench NOTE: Enter lengths recorded on pages 27, 28, and 79.

LEGS (4)   SIDE RAILS (2)

UPPER LEG SUPPORTS (4)   SIDE RAILS (2)

How Much Overhang?
An overhang at the edge of your bench comes in handy for clamping project pieces and accessories. I built my bench with a 3" overhang on all sides.

My Cutlist: EZ Workbench

Cut all pieces from 2x4 dimensional lumber.

LEGS (4)

length:
length:

length:
length:

UPPER LEG SUPPORTS (4)

length:
length:

length:
length:

LOWER LEG SUPPORTS (4)

length:
length:

length:
length:

LEFT SIDE RAILS (2)

length:

length:

RIGHT SIDE RAILS (2)

length:

length:

CENTER RAILS (2)

length:

length:

STRETCHERS (4)

length:

length:

length:

length:

Cut Boards to Size

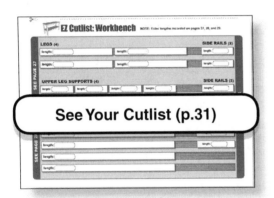

See Your Cutlist (p.31)

Whenever I build a project that has a lot of different pieces, I like to cut the boards to size first. This not only keeps my project better organized, but makes it easier to cut similar pieces exactly the same length—which is often more important than the actual length itself.

On page 31 you'll find a cutting diagram showing all the individual components of your workbench, and a place to enter the board lengths you chose earlier in this plan. An average size workbench calls for approximately six 2x4 boards (8-ft length). However, I recommend buying an extra board or two in case you make a cutting mistake (it happens to all of us!).

Cutting Tips & Tricks

Speed Square
A plastic rafter square (speed square) makes a nice cutting guide for your circular saw. I like to clamp the square and keep both hands on the saw.

Safe Stop
Always let the blade come to a *complete stop* before moving the saw away from the cut (a blade will continue spinning for several seconds after it stops).

Gang Up Boards
The fewer cuts you make, the fewer chances for mistakes. That's why I like to "gang up" same-size project pieces and cut them all in one swoop.

Drill Pilot Holes

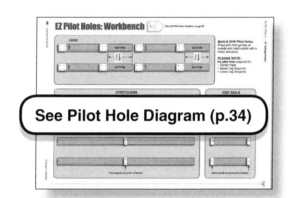

See Pilot Hole Diagram (p.34)

Drilling pilot holes can be a time-consuming job—especially if you leave the task for each stage of the construction. I've found it's much easier to mark and drill pilot holes in *advance,* just after cutting all the project pieces to size.

This not only speeds up the assembly process, but also makes it much easier to measure and mark pilot hole locations—when the boards are laid out on a flat surface within easy reach.

On page 34 you'll find a diagram showing pilot hole locations for each piece of the project. Be sure to use the EZ Pilot Hole Guides (page 79) to help you align the location of the holes.

EZ Pilot Hole Guides

The *location* of the pilot hole is just as important as the hole itself. If it's not in the right place, you can easily ruin a project by splitting the fragile edges of the boards you're trying to join.

That's why I've included a set of pilot hole guides (page 79) to make the task easy.
You can cut the templates directly from this book, and then line them up along the end of each board. I like to use an ice pick or a woodworker's awl to mark the locations. This will also create a nice starter hole for inserting your drill bit.

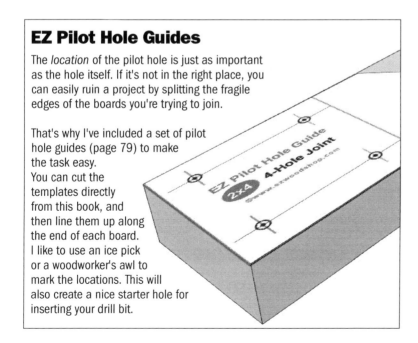

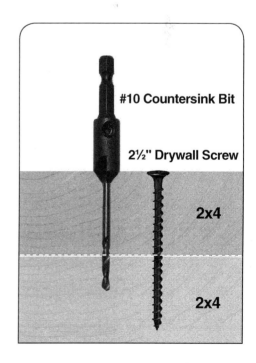

#10 Countersink Bit

2½" Drywall Screw

2x4

2x4

Pilot Hole Diagram: EZ Workbench

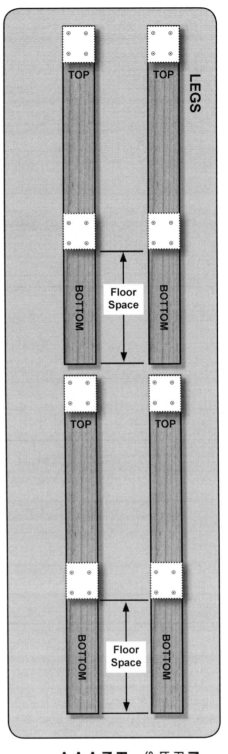

LEGS

TOP · TOP

BOTTOM · BOTTOM

Floor Space

TOP · TOP

BOTTOM · BOTTOM

Floor Space

Mark & Drill Pilot Holes
Place pilot hole guides on boards and mark points with a sharp tool (awl).

PLEASE NOTE:
No pilot hole required for:
- Center Rails
- Upper Leg Supports
- Lower Leg Supports

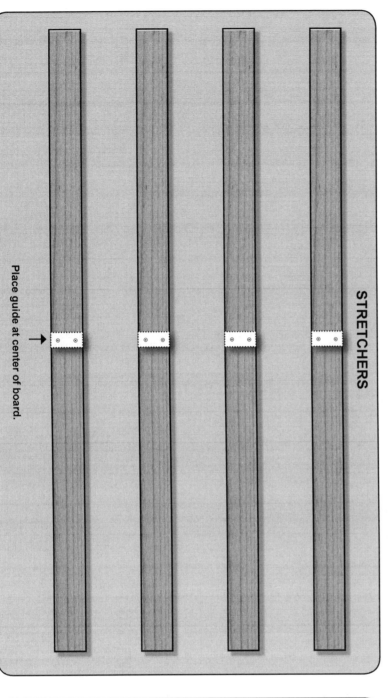

STRETCHERS

Place guide at center of board. →

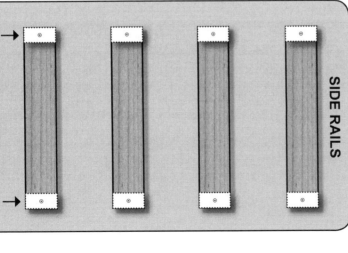

SIDE RAILS

→ Place guide at each end of board. →

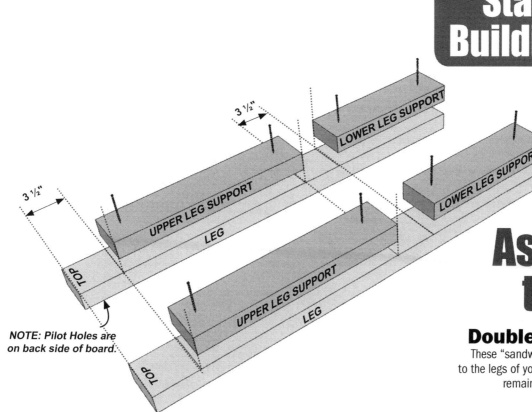

3 ½"

3 ½"

UPPER LEG SUPPORT
LEG

LOWER LEG SUPPORT

UPPER LEG SUPPORT
LEG

LOWER LEG SUPPORT

TOP

TOP

NOTE: Pilot Holes are on back side of board.

Assemble the Legs

Double the Strength!
These "sandwich" joints add super strength to the legs of your bench. Plus, they make the remaining assembly quick and easy.

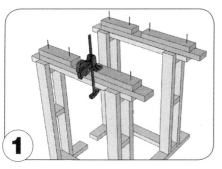

① Set Up
For best results, use sawhorses (or the EZ Cutting Station) as a work space for assembling the legs and leg supports.

② Glue
Apply glue to one side of the joint, and then place the leg support in position (see above illustration to see where to place supports).

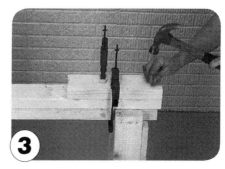

③ Nail
Clamp the leg support to the leg. Drilling a small pilot hole first (1/16" bit) in the support first makes hammering easy.

EZ TIPS

Glue & Nail
The real strength in a glue joint comes from the glue, not the fastener. The 6d nail works like a clamp, holding the two boards together while the glue dries.

——————————— **6d 2" Nail**

(ACTUAL SIZE)

Stubborn Nail?
The easiest way to hammer nails in 2x4s is to drill a small pilot hole first. Use a 1/16" bit from your drill bit set and create a hole halfway through the leg support.

——————————— **1/16" Drill Bit**

(ACTUAL SIZE)

2 Stretchers & Rails

Start Driving Screws!

I like to start with the stretcher and rails, mostly because this gives you a basic frame on which you can easily add the other components of the bench. Be sure to build **two of the frames** you see here—one for the upper part of your bench, one for the lower.

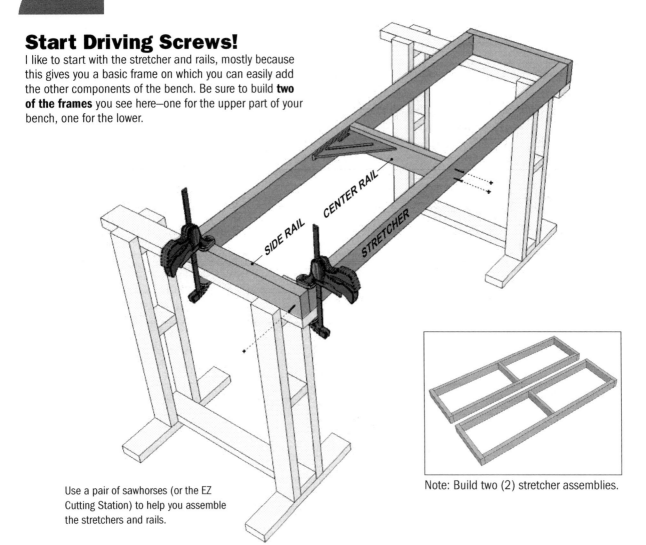

SIDE RAIL   CENTER RAIL   STRETCHER

Use a pair of sawhorses (or the EZ Cutting Station) to help you assemble the stretchers and rails.

Note: Build two (2) stretcher assemblies.

Attach Rear Legs

Bring it Together!

Here's the step where your bench starts looking like a real bench! I like to do this part of the assembly on the floor, with the legs facing up. This lets me drive the screws from above, which is always easier than working from the side.

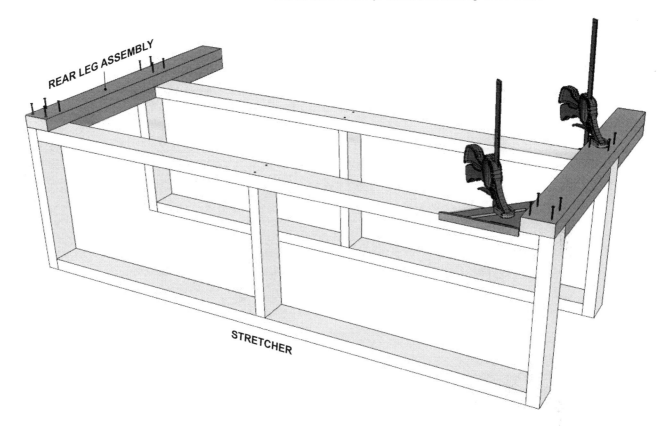

REAR LEG ASSEMBLY

STRETCHER

Work From Above

Sometimes it's easier to drive screws from *above* rather than from the side. That's why I like to attach my first set of legs with the bench turned on its side.

Double-Check for Square

Before driving any screws, make sure the legs are square to the stretchers. After all the nudging is complete, clamp everything down, and then drive the screws.

4 Attach Front Legs

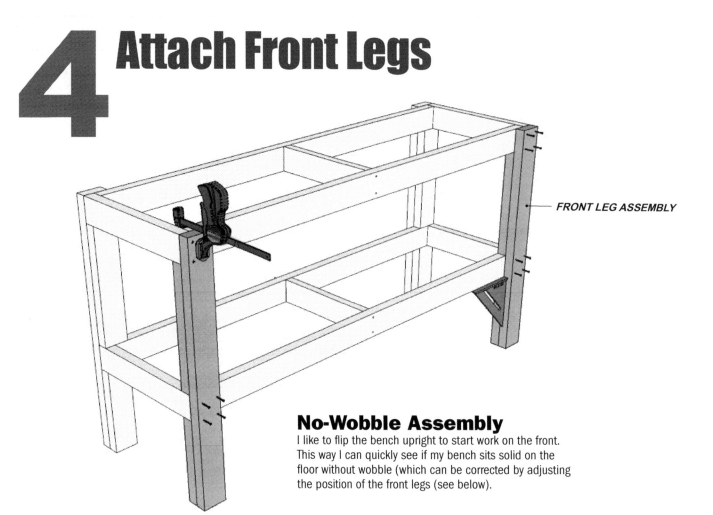

FRONT LEG ASSEMBLY

No-Wobble Assembly

I like to flip the bench upright to start work on the front. This way I can quickly see if my bench sits solid on the floor without wobble (which can be corrected by adjusting the position of the front legs (see below).

Flip the Bench Upright

This will give you a chance to check for noticeable wobble before driving the final screws into place. First "dry assemble" the front legs into position, using a few clamps to hold everything together. Then check for square along the lower stretcher and the lower section of the leg (see photo at right).

Double-Check for Square

Push the legs and stretchers snug against your square and then re-tighten the clamps. If you notice any wobble, try nudging a front leg one direction or another until the entire bench feels solid on the floor. Once you're happy with the results, clamp everything down securely and drive the screws in place.

Attach Top 5

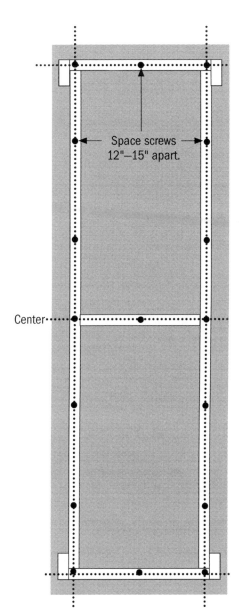

Space screws 12"–15" apart.

Center

1-1/4" Drywall Screws

The coarse thread of a drywall screw is perfect for joining boards made of soft pine. This size should work okay for both ½" and ¾" plywood panels.

ACTUAL SIZE

Glue?

I prefer *not* to glue the top, just in case I need to replace the plywood sometime in the future.

Time to Add a Top!

You have plenty of choices for a bench top—plywood, hardboard, particle board, and even metal. Obviously your choice should reflect the type of work you plan to do, but I've found that ½"-thick plywood makes a nice top for medium-duty work. It's both easy to cut and less expensive than other materials. For benches that demand more strength and stability, I use ¾"-thick plywood.

The only tricky part about attaching the top is figuring out where to drive the screws. That's because the bench top overhang hides the boards you need to drive screws into (stretchers and rails). Not to worry—an adjustable square makes easy work of marking pilot hole locations along the edge of your bench top. Here's how:

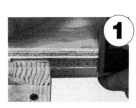

1 Align Top Over Stretchers and Rails
Extend your adjustable square to whatever distance you chose for the overhang (see page 29, 30). Then walk around all sides of the bench, using the square to position the overhang so it is consistent on all sides.

2 Draw Center Line
Extend the square an *additional* 1½". This will place the end of your square directly over center of the stretchers and rails below. Then use the square to draw a line around all sides of the bench (and through center).

3 Mark Pilot Holes
No need for perfection here—just try to get the pilot holes spaced approximately 12"–15" apart. I like to use an ice pick or an awl to mark the holes.

NEXT STEPS
Add a Lower Shelf

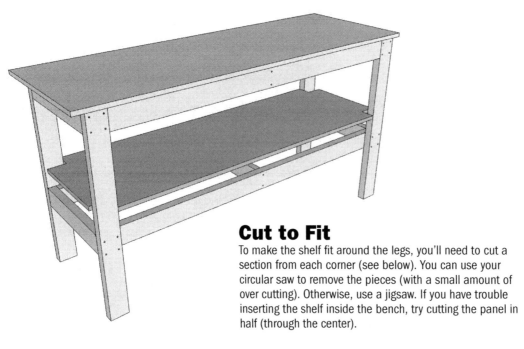

Cut to Fit

To make the shelf fit around the legs, you'll need to cut a section from each corner (see below). You can use your circular saw to remove the pieces (with a small amount of over cutting). Otherwise, use a jigsaw. If you have trouble inserting the shelf inside the bench, try cutting the panel in half (through the center).

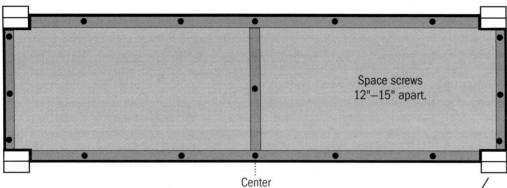

Space screws 12"–15" apart.

Center

1-1/4" Drywall Screws

The coarse thread of a drywall screw is perfect for joining boards made of soft pine. This size should work okay for both ½" and ¾" plywood panels.

(ACTUAL SIZE)

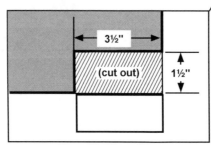

3½"

(cut out)

1½"

Close-Up View of Corner

Glue?

I prefer *not* to glue the lower shelf, just in case I need to replace the plywood sometime in the future.

Build a Side Table

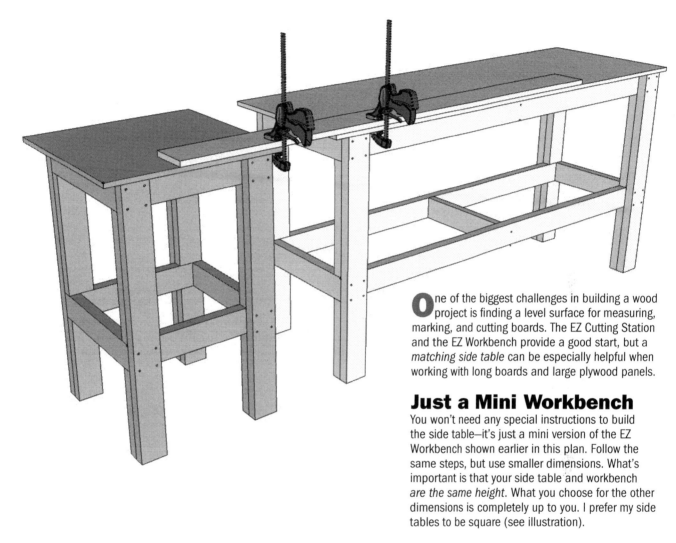

One of the biggest challenges in building a wood project is finding a level surface for measuring, marking, and cutting boards. The EZ Cutting Station and the EZ Workbench provide a good start, but a *matching side table* can be especially helpful when working with long boards and large plywood panels.

Just a Mini Workbench

You won't need any special instructions to build the side table—it's just a mini version of the EZ Workbench shown earlier in this plan. Follow the same steps, but use smaller dimensions. What's important is that your side table and workbench *are the same height*. What you choose for the other dimensions is completely up to you. I prefer my side tables to be square (see illustration).

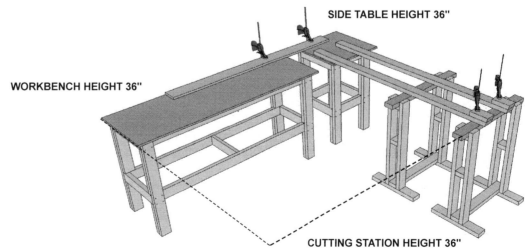

SIDE TABLE HEIGHT 36"

WORKBENCH HEIGHT 36"

CUTTING STATION HEIGHT 36"

Joinery Guide: Legs

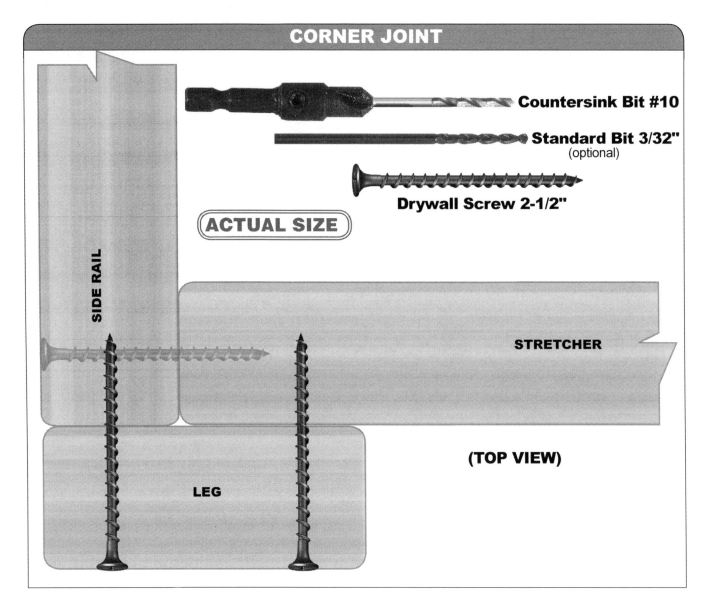

CORNER JOINT

Countersink Bit #10

Standard Bit 3/32"
(optional)

Drywall Screw 2-1/2"

ACTUAL SIZE

SIDE RAIL

STRETCHER

LEG

(TOP VIEW)

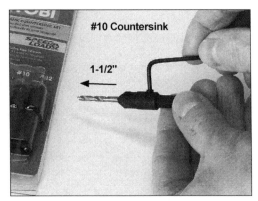

#10 Countersink

1-1/2"

Adjusting the Countersink Bit

Most countersink bits include a hex-key screw that allows you to extend the length of the bit. A #10 countersink extended to its maximum length will create a pilot hole that passes completely through the thickness of one 2x4, and lightly break the surface of the adjoining board. In most cases, this should be sufficient for driving screws. However, if you have any trouble making the screw go completely into both boards, try re-drilling a deeper pilot hole using a standard 3/32" drill bit.

Trouble driving screws?
Try drilling a deeper pilot hole using a standard 3/32" bit.

Joinery Guide: Top & Shelf

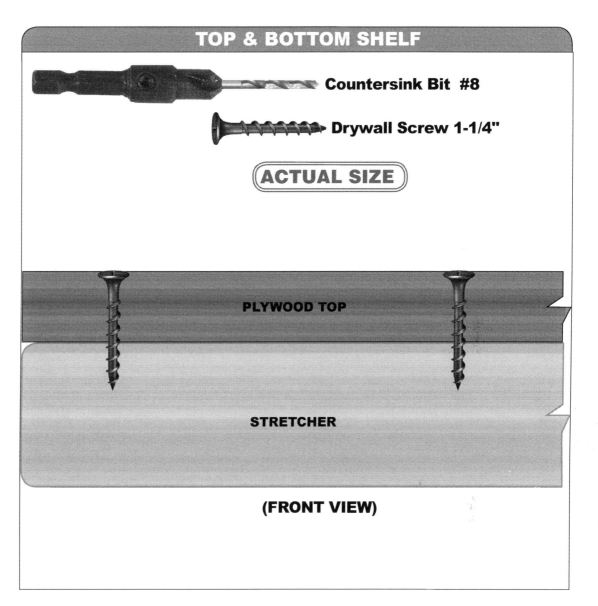

TOP & BOTTOM SHELF

Countersink Bit #8

Drywall Screw 1-1/4"

ACTUAL SIZE

PLYWOOD TOP

STRETCHER

(FRONT VIEW)

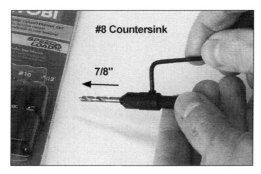

#8 Countersink

7/8"

Adjusting the Countersink Bit

When mounting a plywood top, I like to extend the countersink bit about 7/8" beyond the tapered head. This creates a nice pilot hole through both boards and a recessed countersink hole for the head of the screw.

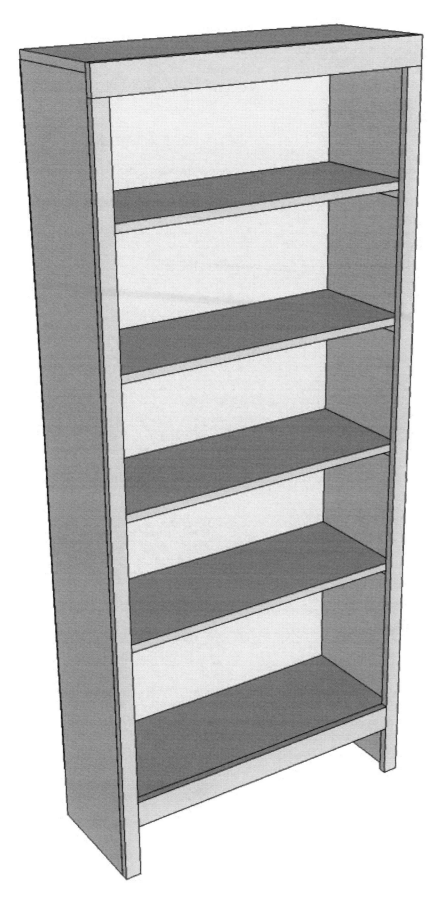

Solid Wood
Bookcase

Who *doesn't* need a bookcase? It's one of the most practical and useful pieces f furniture you'll ever own. And that's exactly hy I've included a bookcase in this series. est part is that bookcases are fairly easy to uild, given a few basic skills under your belt which you now have after building the cutting ation and workbench!).

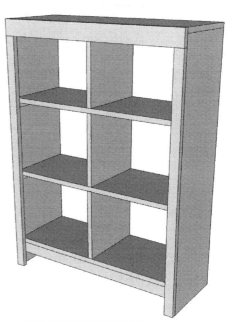

simple 1X12 construction

Bookcase: Anatomy

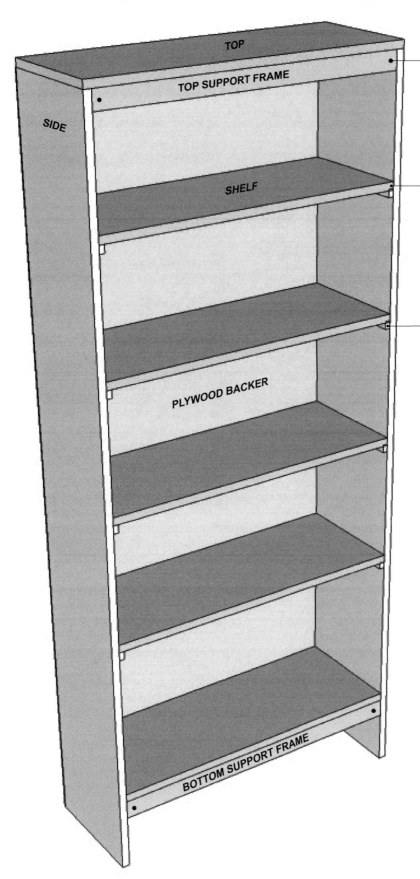

TOP

TOP SUPPORT FRAME

SIDE

SHELF

PLYWOOD BACKER

BOTTOM SUPPORT FRAME

Support Frames

There's nothing worse than a wobbly (and unsafe) bookcase. The support frames (see below) help keep your bookcase tough and rigid. A support frame consists of two *stretchers* and two *rails* (see below).

Shelves

1x12 boards are perfect for bookcase shelves. They are tough, durable, and provide just enough depth for most sizes of books.

Cleats

Cleats provide a small footing that supports a shelf at each end. That means no dados, no biscuits, and no complicated joinery tools are required. It's one of the easiest ways to build a bookcase.

Solid Wood Construction

If you've ever bought a cheap bookcase, you already know what's better about solid wood construction. This project that will last a lifetime—and then some!

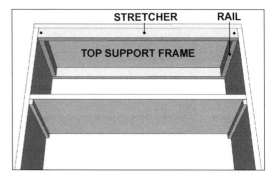

STRETCHER   **RAIL**

TOP SUPPORT FRAME

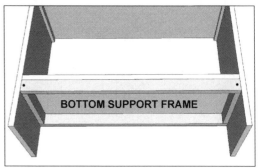

BOTTOM SUPPORT FRAME

Getting Started

For those who have already built the EZ Cutting Station or the EZ Workbench (included in the series), most of the tools and materials listed below should be things you now have in the shop.

What's new in this project is the type of boards you'll be using. Instead of shopping for 2x4 studs, you'll be buying boards a few aisles down—where home improvement stores keep a large selection "1x" boards stacked vertically in the aisle. For this bookcase design, I used *1x12 common pine* for the sides, top, and shelves. I chose poplar for the 1x2 support frames and the molding, since poplar has a denser grain and tends to be more straight and square than pine. You can also use other types of hardwoods for the support frames and molding, like maple and oak.

Tools You'll Need

Circular Saw

Portable Drill

Hand Clamps (4) 6"

Measuring Tape

Speed Squares 8" 12"

Adjustable Square

Lumber & Hardware

Pine (common) 1x12   Plywood 1/8"

Hardwood 1x2

Hardwood Molding 3/4 x 1/2

Drill Bit Set

Countersink Bit Set #6 - #8 - #10 - #12

Drywall Screws 1¼" 1"

Wire Nails ¾"

Your Design

My Choice for Bookcase Height: _____

Choose Bookcase Height

Make sure you (and other family members) can safely reach what's on the shelf. Use the chart on this page to estimate the best bookcase height for you.

**ADULT REACH
60" - 72"**

**CHILD REACH
36" - 48"**

Choose Shelf Span

No-Sag Maximum Shelf Spans

There's nothing worse than a bookcase with sagging shelves! Use the chart below to find the best length for shelves made of oak, pine, plywood, and MDF.

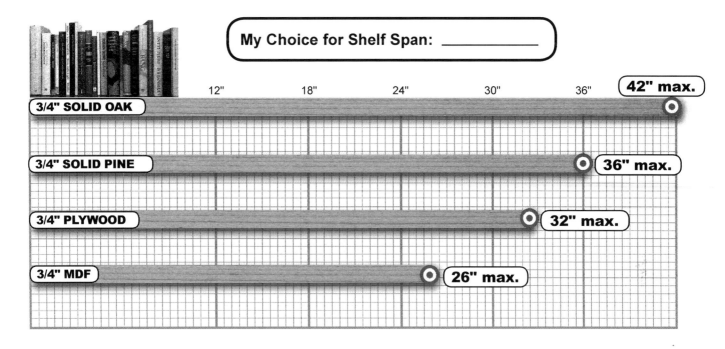

My Choice for Shelf Span: _____

	12"	18"	24"	30"	36"	
3/4" SOLID OAK						42" max.
3/4" SOLID PINE					36" max.	
3/4" PLYWOOD				32" max.		
3/4" MDF		26" max.				

Choose Shelf Height

Make Sure Your Books Fit!

Before you start building your bookcase, take a look at your book collection and decide how many tall shelves you'll need (for the largest books) and how many short shelves you'll need for the paperbacks.

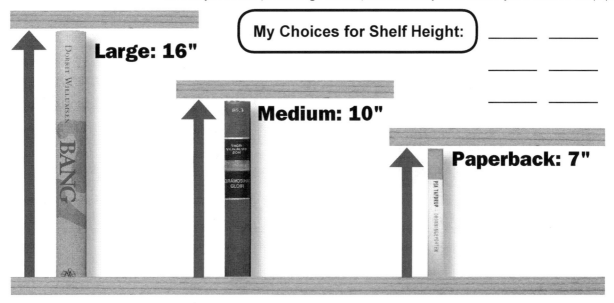

My Choices for Shelf Height: _____ _____

_____ _____

_____ _____

Large: 16"

Medium: 10"

Paperback: 7"

Make Your Cutlist

Bookcase Top

Find Length for TOP

Shelf Span (see page 49) **+** 3/4" Side Thickness (left) **+** 3/4" Side Thickness (right) **=** Top Length

Enter on EZ Cutlist (p.52)

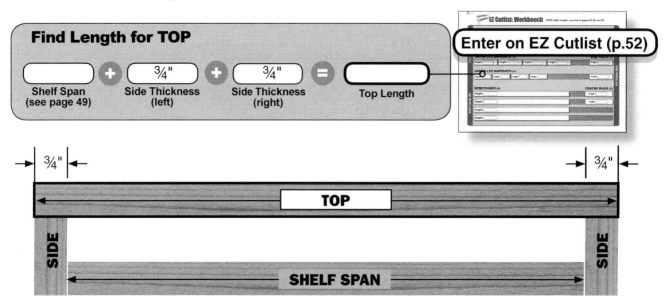

Bookcase Sides

Find Length for SIDES

Bookcase Height (see page 48) **−** 3/4" Top Thickness **=** Side Length

Enter on EZ Cutlist (p.52)

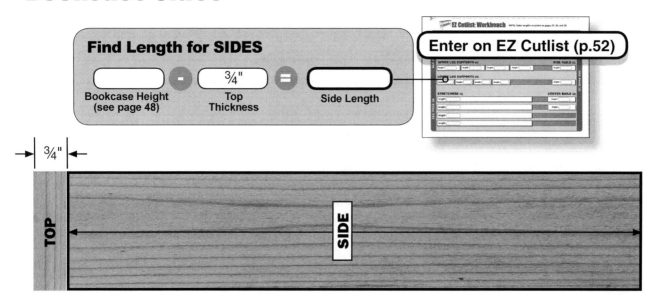

Make Your Cutlist

Bookcase Shelves

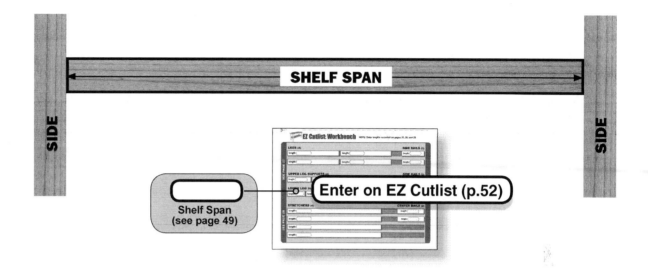

SHELF SPAN

SIDE

SIDE

Shelf Span
(see page 49)

Enter on EZ Cutlist (p.52)

Support Frames (Stretchers & Rails)

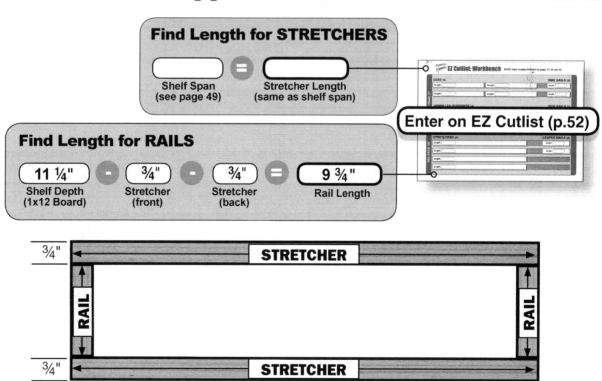

Find Length for STRETCHERS

Shelf Span
(see page 49)

=

Stretcher Length
(same as shelf span)

Enter on EZ Cutlist (p.52)

Find Length for RAILS

11 ¼"	-	¾"	-	¾"	=	9 ¾"
Shelf Depth (1x12 Board)		Stretcher (front)		Stretcher (back)		Rail Length

¾"

STRETCHER

RAIL

RAIL

¾"

STRETCHER

My Cutlist: EZ Bookcase

SIDE: ⬭

1x12 PINE

SIDE: ⬭

1x12 PINE

SHELF SPAN: ⬭

SHELF SPAN: ⬭

1x12 PINE

SHELF SPAN: ⬭

SHELF SPAN: ⬭

SHELF SPAN: ⬭

TOP: ⬭

1x12 PINE

TOP FRAME

STRETCHER: ⬭

STRETCHER: ⬭

RAIL: ⬭   RAIL: ⬭

1x2 POPLAR

BOTTOM FRAME

STRETCHER: ⬭

STRETCHER: ⬭

RAIL: ⬭   RAIL: ⬭

1x2 POPLAR

CLEATS (8)

All cleats this length: ⬭

1x2 POPLAR

Cut Boards to Size

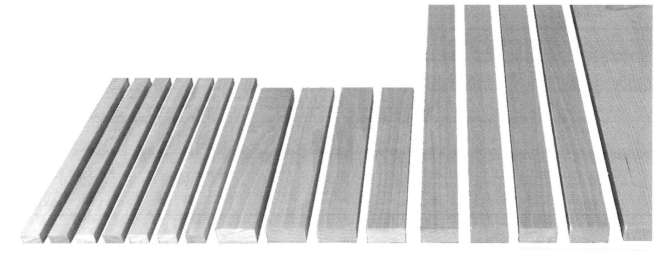

Whenever I build a project that has a lot of pieces, I like to first cut the boards down to the sizes I need. This not only keeps my project better organized, but also makes it easier keep same-size pieces *exactly the same length*—which is often more important than the actual length itself.

On page 52 you'll find a diagram showing all the pieces that make up the bookcase, along with the lengths you'll need to cut for each piece. Take this page with you to the lumber store, and keep it nearby in the shop when it's time to cut the boards. It will help keep your project organized, efficient, and accurate.

Keep in mind that a warped or twisted board will cause you trouble later on during assembly. If after cutting your boards you discover one piece is crooked, cut a new piece from another board.

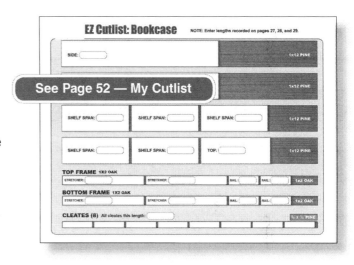

See Page 52 — My Cutlist

Cutting Tips & Tricks

Use Speed Square

A plastic rafter square (speed square) makes a nice cutting guide for your circular saw. I like to clamp the square and keep both hands on the saw.

Let Blade Stop

Always let the blade come to a *complete stop* before moving the saw away from the cut (a blade will continue spinning for several seconds after it stops).

Gang Up Boards

The fewer cuts you make, the fewer chances for mistakes. That's why I like to "gang up" same-size project pieces and cut them all in one swoop.

Drill Pilot Holes

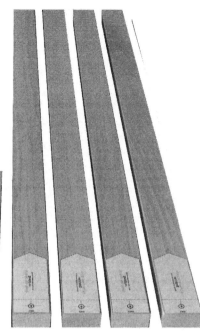

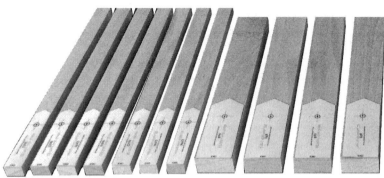

Drilling a pilot hole can sometimes make a board shift and move out of position, even with the tightest grip you can muster from a clamp. That's why I prefer to mark and drill pilot holes *before assembly,* just after cutting all my project pieces to size.

This also makes it easier to measure and mark the pilot hole locations—while the boards are still laid out flat on your work table.

On page 55 you'll find a diagram that shows where to drill pilot holes on each piece of the project. The EZ Pilot Hole Guides (page 85) will to help you align the location of the holes, and prevent splitting the edges of your project pieces.

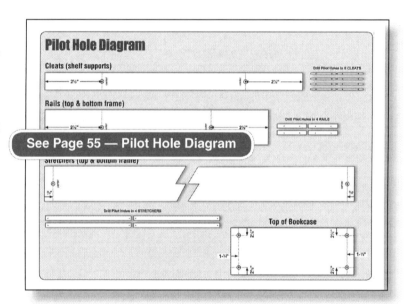

Pilot Hole Diagram

Cleats (shelf supports)

Rails (top & bottom frame)

See Page 55 — Pilot Hole Diagram

Stretchers (top & bottom frame)

Top of Bookcase

#8 Countersink Bit

1¼" Drywall Screw

1x2

1x2

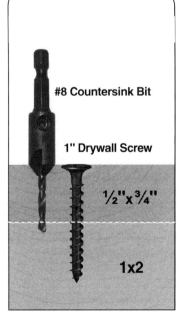

#8 Countersink Bit

1" Drywall Screw

½" x ¾"

1x2

EZ Pilot Hole Guides......page 85

The *location* of a pilot hole is just as important as the hole itself. If it's not in the right place, you can easily ruin a project by splitting the fragile edges of the boards you're trying to join.

That's why I've included a set of pilot hole guides (page 85) to make the task easy. Cut the templates directly out of this book, and then line them up along the end of each board. I like to use an ice pick or a woodworker's awl to mark the screw locations. This will also create a nice starter hole for inserting your drill bit.

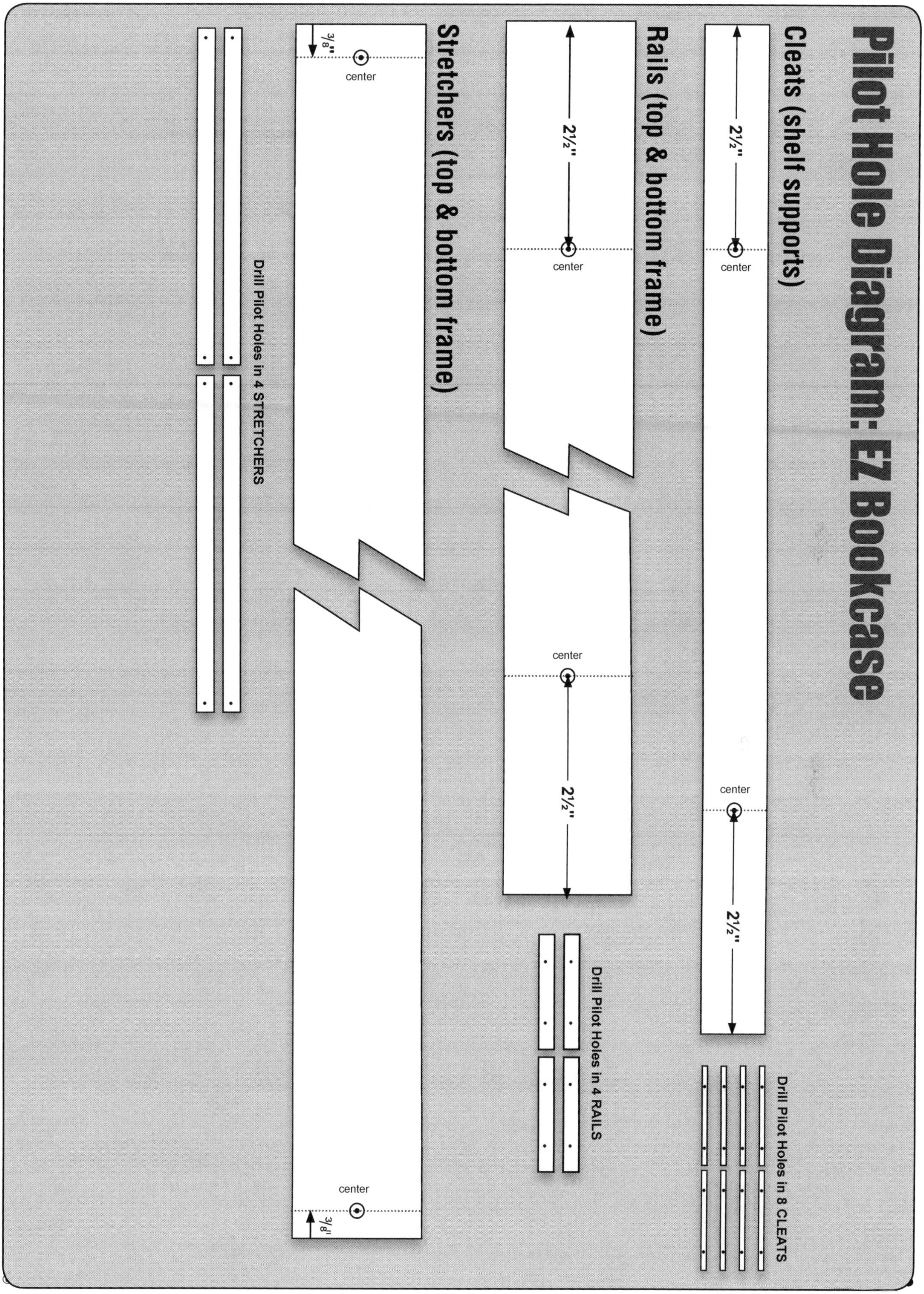

Pilot Hole Diagram: EZ Bookcase

Cleats (shelf supports)

2½"
center

center

2½"

Drill Pilot Holes in **8 CLEATS**

Rails (top & bottom frame)

2½"
center

center

2½"

Drill Pilot Holes in **4 RAILS**

Stretchers (top & bottom frame)

3/8"
center

center
3/8"

Drill Pilot Holes in **4 STRETCHERS**

Support Frames

Start Building!

Build the Foundation

The support frames help ensure that your bookcase goes together straight, square, and strong. That's why it's important to get these pieces assembled with as much precision as possible—making sure the corners meet at precise right angles and all edges are flush to each other. Use your EZ Cutting Station or your EZ Workbench to provide a flat, square surface for completing the assembly (see right).

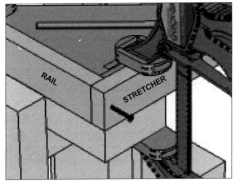

Use your square to make sure the corners are at precise right angles. Apply glue, clamp everything down tight, and drive the screws. If the screw is being stubborn, try drilling a deeper pilot hole using a 3/32" drill bit.

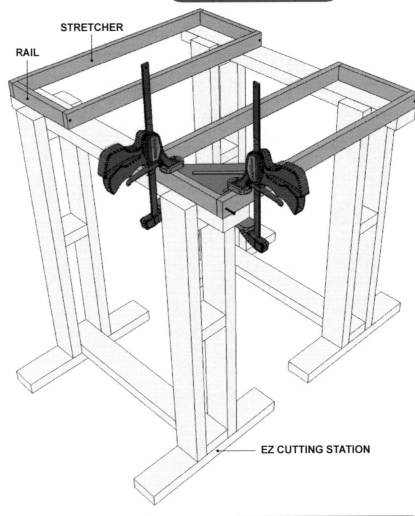

STRETCHER

RAIL

EZ CUTTING STATION

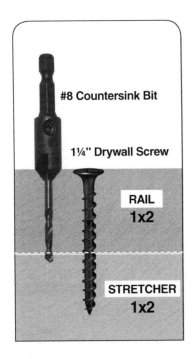

#8 Countersink Bit

1¼" Drywall Screw

RAIL
1x2

STRETCHER
1x2

Add Glue First

Apply glue between the rail and stretcher (one side only). Then clamp and screw.

rail

stretcher

GLUE

Use Drywall Screws

1¼"

ACTUAL SIZE

Stubborn Screw?

Try re-drilling the pilot hole with a 3/32" bit.

3/32" Drill Bit

Mark Guidelines for Cleats

2

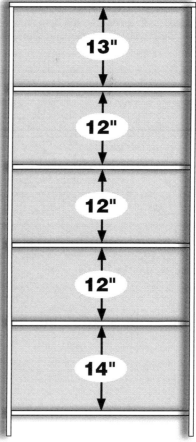

Straight & Level

It's important to get these guidelines draw accurately, since the location of the cleats determine how straight your shelves will look in the cabinet. That's why I like to mark both sides of the bookcase at the same time (see above). This ensures that the shelves are perfectly level across the width of the bookcase.

Shelf Height?

The layout diagram at right shows my choices for shelf height, but you can easily alter the design to fit your needs (see page 49).

I chose 13" for the top shelf height—which gives me a little extra space for a decorative trim piece I'll attach along the top later. The middle shelves are all 12" apart—which is a nice height for most of the books I own.

I gave the bottom shelf a little extra space (14") to allow for some of my larger, oversized books and photo albums.

Design Your Own?

See page 48 for how-to tips on creating your own bookcase design.

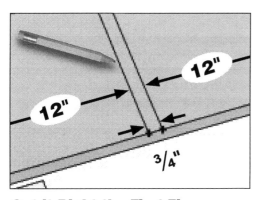

Get it Right the First Time
Carefully mark the shelf locations to ensure a straight and square bookcase.

3 Attach Shelf Cleats

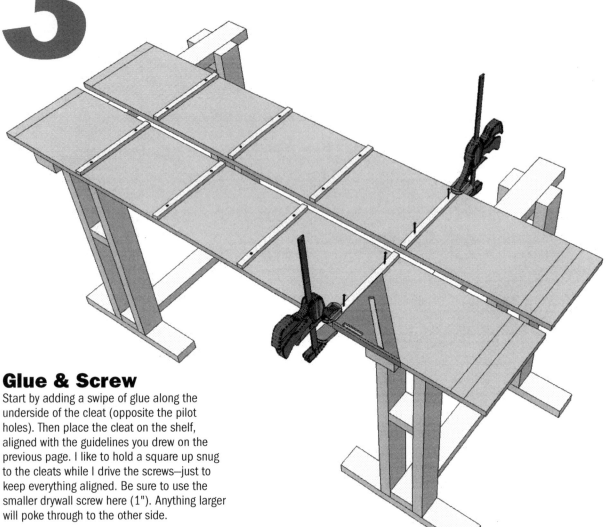

Glue & Screw

Start by adding a swipe of glue along the underside of the cleat (opposite the pilot holes). Then place the cleat on the shelf, aligned with the guidelines you drew on the previous page. I like to hold a square up snug to the cleats while I drive the screws—just to keep everything aligned. Be sure to use the smaller drywall screw here (1"). Anything larger will poke through to the other side.

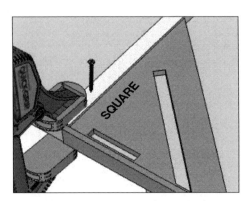

Use your square to keep the cleat at a right angle while you drive the screw. I like to grip the square with one hand, and use my other hand to hold the drill.

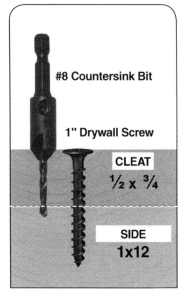

#8 Countersink Bit

1" Drywall Screw

CLEAT
½ x ¾

SIDE
1x12

Add Glue First

Apply glue between the cleat and the bookcase side. Clamp and drive screws.

CLEAT
SIDE — GLUE

Use Drywall Screws

1"

ACTUAL SIZE

Attach Supports

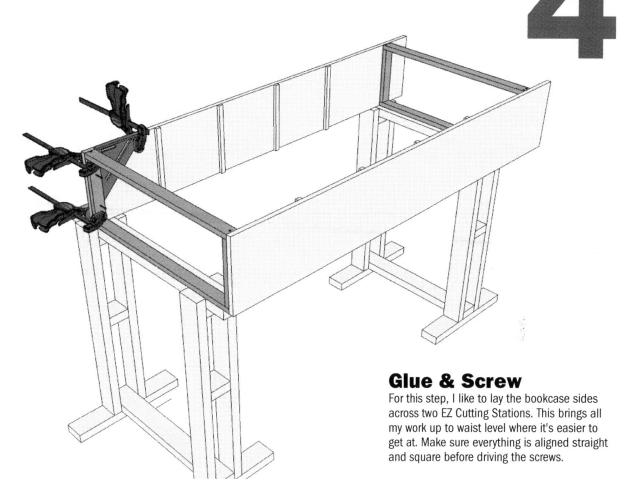

Glue & Screw

For this step, I like to lay the bookcase sides across two EZ Cutting Stations. This brings all my work up to waist level where it's easier to get at. Make sure everything is aligned straight and square before driving the screws.

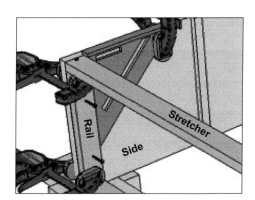

Use your square to make sure the joints are at perfect right angles. If you get this part of the assembly right, the rest of the bookcase project will be smooth sailing!

Add Glue First

Apply glue between the rail and the bookcase side. Then drive screws.

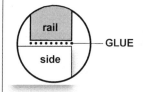

Use Drywall Screws

1¼"

ACTUAL SIZE

5 Glue Middle Shelf

Glue & Clamp Shelf

Although it's not necessary to glue *all* of the shelves in place, it's a good idea to glue at least one shelf to provide some extra strength and support for the overall structure. Choose a shelf location near the middle of the bookcase, then glue and clamp the shelf to the cleat. Let dry overnight.

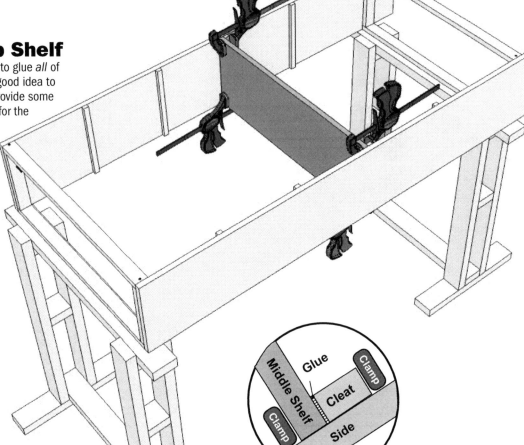

Mark Center

Make a small mark on the side of the bookcase to reveal the location of the center shelf. You'll need this guide for attaching the plywood back in a later step (see page 62).

Glue & Clamp

Apply glue between the middle shelf and the cleat. Clamp and let dry overnight.

IMPORTANT NOTE:
Adding a Center Divider?

If you plan to customize this bookcase plan by adding a center divider, you'll need to **glue all horizontal shelves in place to complete this step.**

See page 66 for more on creating a custom design.

Attach Top

6

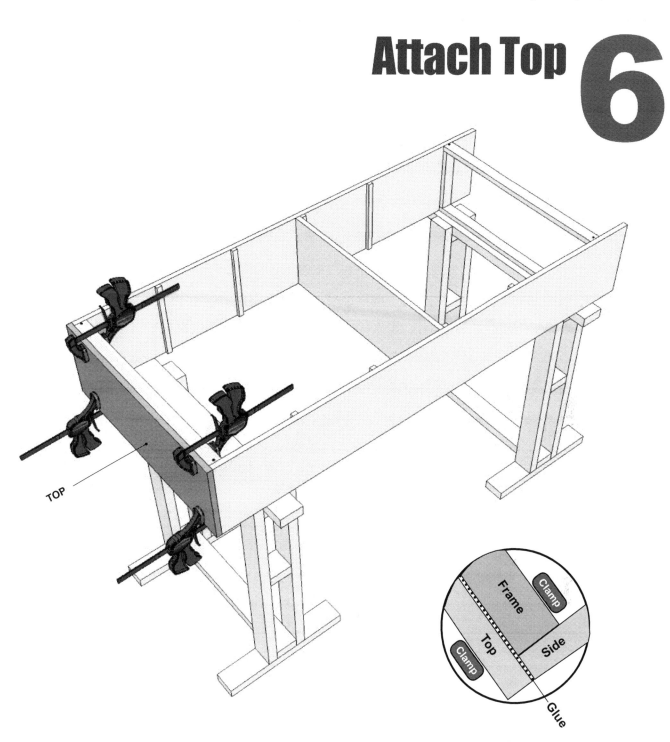

TOP

Glue & Clamp

 Move your cutting station back a few inches and try positioning the top over the support frame. If everything lines up okay, set the top aside and apply glue along the edge of the frame. Then clamp the top at all four edges (see illustration).

7 Cut Plywood Back

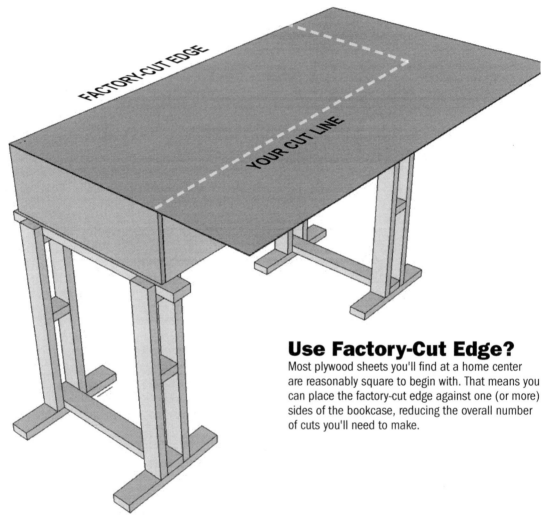

FACTORY-CUT EDGE

YOUR CUT LINE

Use Factory-Cut Edge?

Most plywood sheets you'll find at a home center are reasonably square to begin with. That means you can place the factory-cut edge against one (or more) sides of the bookcase, reducing the overall number of cuts you'll need to make.

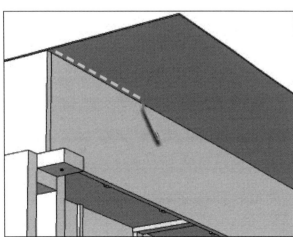

No Need to Measure

The best way to determine where to cut your plywood is to simply trace the outline of the bookcase directly on the panel (from the underside). Be sure the panel is aligned flush and square along the edges.

Attach Plywood Back

Glued-in Shelf Line

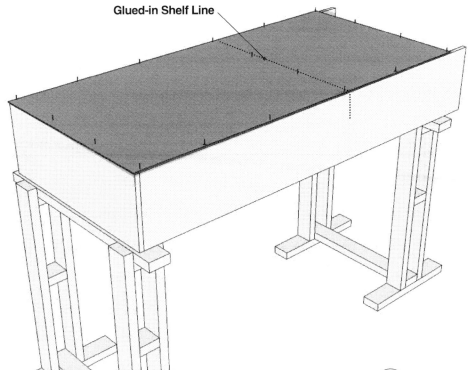

Space nails approximately 12" apart.

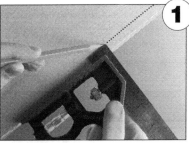

1 Draw Guideline
Set your carpenter's square to 3/8" and draw a line completely around the perimeter. Make sure the square is snug against the side while you pull it along. This will give you a guideline perfectly centered over the 1x12 just below. Then mark a spot where you will drive each nail—every 12" should do the trick.

2 Apply Glue
Before nailing down the back, apply a bead of glue around the perimeter and across the middle shelf. Gluing will help add stability and overall strength to your bookcase. Be sure to have a damp rag ready—the glue will probably ooze out of the joint and start running down the sides of your bookcase.

3 Drive Nails
Drive a ¾" wire nail at each location you marked in step 1. If you prefer to hide the nails before adding a finish to the project, drive the head just under the surface using a *nail punch* or *nail set*.

Congratulations!

It's a Bookcase!

Now simply insert the remaining shelves, letting them rest freely on the cleats you installed earlier. Don't worry if some shelves have a stubborn fit—I have a few work a rounds to solve the problem (see below).

Shelf Won't Fit?

Even with our best attempts to measure accurately, sometimes things just don't fit as planned (usually from inconsistencies in dimensional lumber). As you can see in the photo above, a couple of my shelves were too long to fit comfortably inside the cabinet.

Solution: Relocate

First try placing the shelf in *another location* of the bookcase. Sometimes this alone will solve the problem (my stubborn shelf fit better towards the bottom than the top.

Solution: Sand

You can also shorten the length of a shelf by sanding one edge using a fairly coarse sandpaper grade (60# to 80#). Be sure to re-check the fit often. Sometimes all it takes is a few passes with a sanding block to get the right fit (don't make it too short!).

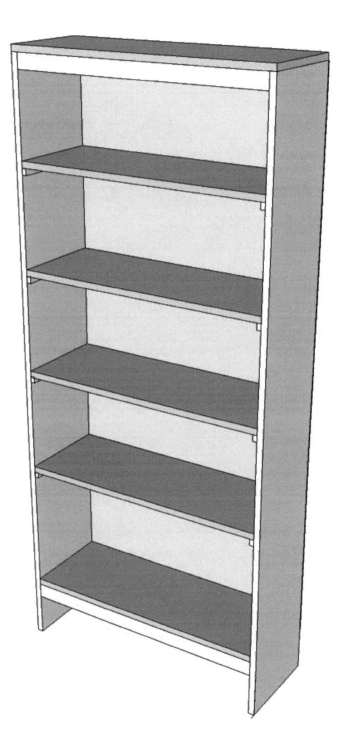

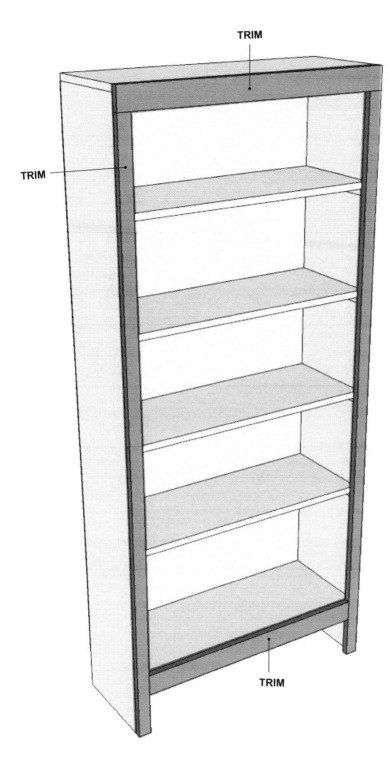

TRIM

TRIM

TRIM

Dress it Up!

One of the easiest way to improve the appearance of your bookcase is to add a few pieces of molding around the edges. The molding does a nice job of hiding unsightly joints, fasteners, or anything else you want to conceal. With my bookcase (see left), I kept the design fairly simple by attaching a wide piece of molding across the top and bottom (to hide the support frames), and a thinner piece on each side (to hide the shelf cleats).

Make it Your Style!

In the "mill work" department at your local home center, you'll find a nearly endless variety of choices for trim and molding. Some of the more decorative boards can get expensive (most are sold by the foot), but since you'll be buying only a few short lengths, they can still be affordable.

Attaching Trim

Try to avoid using screws or other large fasteners to attach trim to your bookcase. These can easily split the wood and leave large holes that you'll have to fill later. Instead, try using small finish nails to attach trim pieces along the edges. You might also try using a hot glue gun.

NEXT STEPS
Add Center Divider

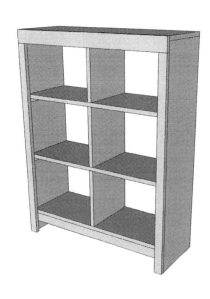

Glue in Place

Here's an easy way to break up your shelf space into small cube sections. Just buy an extra 1x12 board, and then cut pieces to fit the vertical space between shelves. No need to drive screws or nails—simply add a swipe of glue on each end of the divider and set into place. Use a square to make sure everything is lined up correctly, and then let dry overnight. Keep in mind that you'll need to cut away two notches on the **top divider** to accommodate the support frame (see diagram below).

NOTE: This bookcase style requires all shelves to be glued in place. See page 60.

TOP SHELF DIVIDER

DIVIDER

DIVIDER

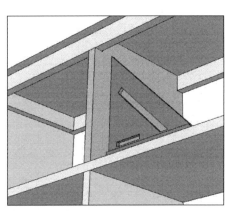

Keep it Square

Be sure to use your speed square when lining up the dividers. I also suggest cutting the pieces a bit larger than needed, and then sand the edges to get a perfect, snug fit.

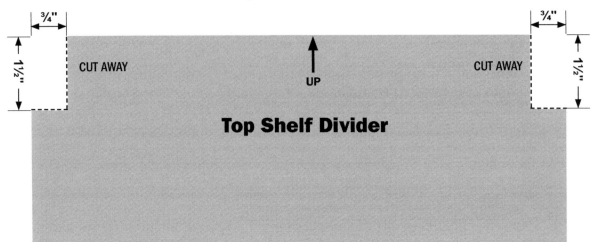

3/4"

1 1/2"

CUT AWAY

UP

3/4"

1 1/2"

CUT AWAY

Top Shelf Divider

Clear Finish

NEXT STEPS
Clear Finish

I've always liked the natural look of pine, but I know that leaving wood unprotected shortens the life of a project. A clear finish offers the best of both worlds—keeping the warm, natural look of the wood while at the same time providing the protection pine needs to last a lifetime. See my tips below for applying a clear finish on pine.

3 Steps for a Clear Finish

Prepare Wood
After sanding, remove all excess dust. Use a vacuum cleaner, cotton rag, or woodworking "wiping cloth" sold at hardware stores.

Apply Finish
Check the instructions on the can for specifics on how to apply. Then practice on a test board to see how your chosen finish behaves.

Add More Coats
One layer is rarely enough to create a durable finish. Lightly sand and dust between coats. Avoid using steel wool (the residue will rust).

My Top Choices for Clear Finish on Pine

MinWax Poly
This is MinWax's most popular water-base finish. It's a nearly foolproof product that works on just about any kind of surface.

General Finishes
Rated *Best Brush-On* by *Fine Woodworking* magazine, this water-base clear coat has low VOCs—and a low price.

Zinsser Shellac
Shellac is making a comeback of sorts in woodworking. The natural ingredients make it easy on wood—and easy on environment.

NEXT STEPS
Staining Pine

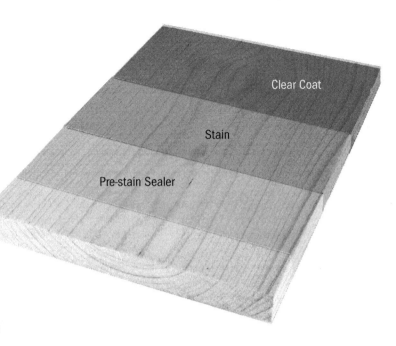

Clear Coat

Stain

Pre-stain Sealer

Staining pine can be tricky. The soft wood is notorious soaking up stain unevenly, leaving stubborn blotches and streaks. Fortunately, there are a few preventative steps you can take to resolve the problem (see below). Keep in mind that a stain add color, but it doesn't really protect the wood. That means you'll need to apply a clear protective finish on top.

Water-base vs Oil-base Stains

For simple wood projects made from pine, I prefer water-base stains over the more toxic oil-base products. Water-base stains have a much lower VOC content, are available in more color choices, and are easy to clean up with soap and water.

3 Steps for Staining Pine

Apply Pre-stain
Start with a pre-stain conditioner to avoid leaving blotches and streaks in pine.

Apply Stain
Take your choice from dozens of colors and shades available at your home center.

Add Top Coat
Protect your completed project from dust, dirt, and scratches with a clear top coat.

My Favorite Products for Staining

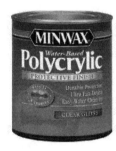

Pre-Stain
A water-base pre-stain is nearly 20 times less toxic than its oil-base cousin. Note: Be sure to use a *water-base stain* with this product.

Stain
At last count, Minwax had 50 different color choices in water-base stains. These are custom-mixed at the counter.

Top Coat
This is Minwax's most popular water-base finish. It's a nearly foolproof finish that works on just about any kind of surface.

Painting Pine

One of the more practical choices for finishing pine is to simply paint the wood. Painting is somewhat less complex than staining, and it's a job that most people are already familiar doing. However, this doesn't mean that painting wood is necessarily quick or easy. A professional-looking paint job takes preparation and patience. See my tips below for applying a paint finish on pine.

Paint

Primer

3 Steps for Painting Pine

Clean Wood
After sanding, remove all excess dust. Use a vacuum cleaner, cotton rag, or woodworking "wiping cloth" sold at hardware stores.

Add Primer
A primer is essential—especially when attempting to cover a soft, porous wood like pine. See page 22 for tips on covering knots.

Apply Paint
One coat is rarely enough. Lightly sand and dust between coats, then use a fine-bristle brush or roller on the final coats.

My Favorite Primer   My Favorite Paints

Zinsser Zero
When painting projects indoors, I look for the lowest VOC rating I can find. Zero sounds good to me.

Rust-Oleum
With reasonably low VOCs, this paint is easy to find at home centers and hardware stores.

Olympic
Olympic is trying to make an environmentally-sound paint, and this one is getting there.

NEXT STEPS

How to Seal Knots in Pine

Leaky, bleeding knots in pine have plagued furniture builders for centuries. The resin is nearly impossible to conceal with common wood finishes. Of course, *if you like the look* of knots in your project you have nothing to worry about. Otherwise you'll need to use a special primer to conceal the knots—especially if you plan to paint).

Seal Knots with Glue

Some builders attempt to seal knots by coating them with epoxy glues. Although epoxy might do the job of permanently sealing the resin inside the knot, the glue will leave a raised bump on the surface of your board, which might be difficult sand.

Shellac-Based Primer

The consensus among most project builders is that the best solution is to use an alcohol-based shellac sealer (B-I-N shellac primer/sealer). Take special note of the "shellac" component here. Other types of primer sealers, like water-base and oil-base sealers, just don't hold up against the resin that will continue to leak from a pine knot.

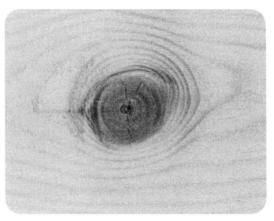

Knots in pine can be tough to seal. Both oil-base and water-base primers usually fail.

Shellac-Base (yes)

The best solution for sealing up stubborn knots in pine is to use an alcohol-based shellac sealer, like B-I-N shellac primer/sealer. Shellac works as an effective barrier between two chemical compounds—like the resin in a pine knot and the pigment in most latex/water-based paints.

Oil-Base (no)

Most people mistakenly assume an oil-base primer will do the trick of sealing up knots. Although these primers might appear to work at the start, the effect is short lived. Eventually the resin from a pine knot will work its way through both the primer and a topcoat.

Water-Base (no)

I can understand the desire to use water-base products. Unfortunately, water-base sealers are nearly useless in containing the resin that will continue to seep out of a pine knot. In fact, the sealer is likely to fail within just a few hours as the resin finds its way to the surface.

EZ Pilot Hole Guides

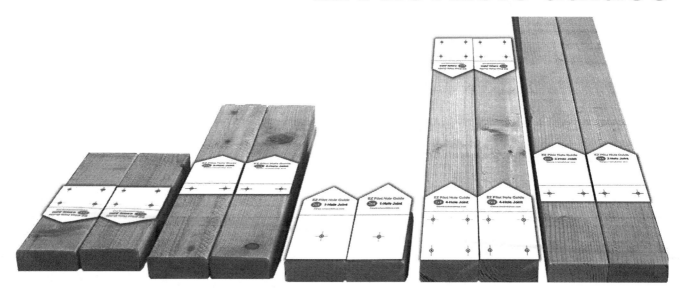

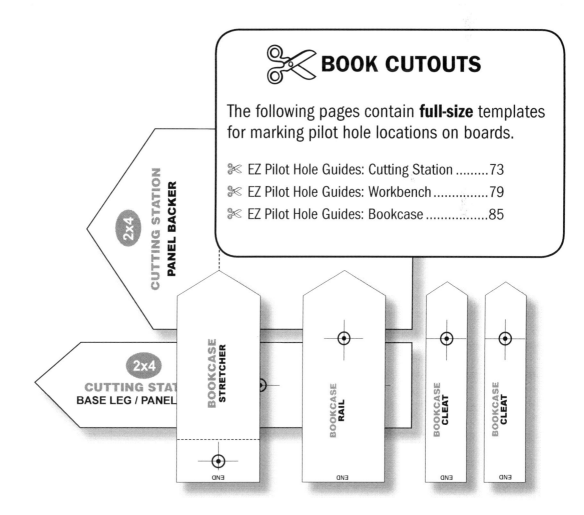

✂ BOOK CUTOUTS

The following pages contain **full-size** templates for marking pilot hole locations on boards.

✂ EZ Pilot Hole Guides: Cutting Station 73
✂ EZ Pilot Hole Guides: Workbench 79
✂ EZ Pilot Hole Guides: Bookcase 85

BOOK CUTOUTS

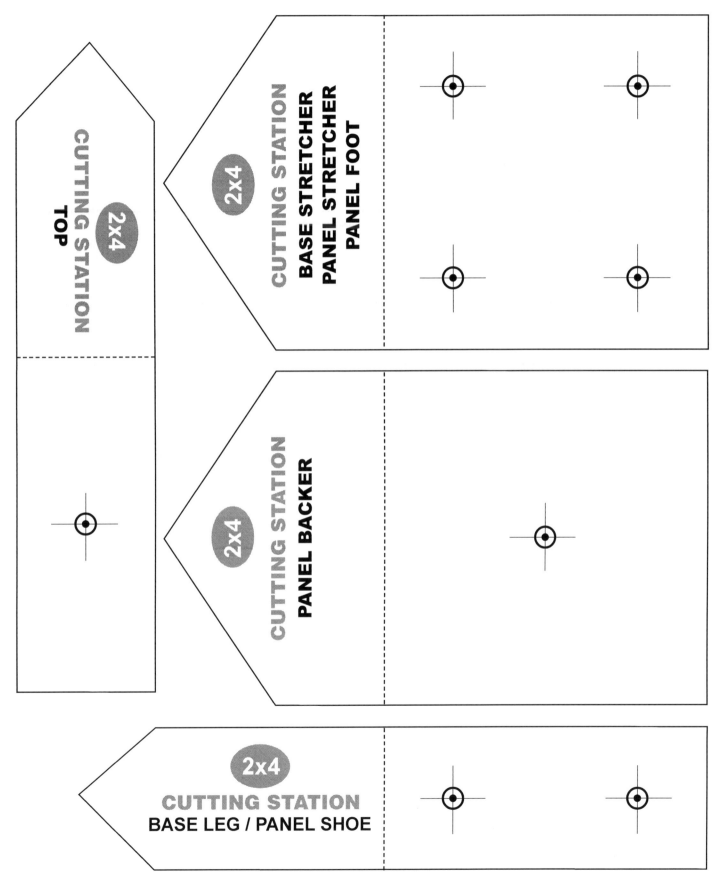

CUTTING STATION
TOP
2x4

CUTTING STATION
BASE STRETCHER
PANEL STRETCHER
PANEL FOOT
2x4

CUTTING STATION
PANEL BACKER
2x4

2x4
CUTTING STATION
BASE LEG / PANEL SHOE

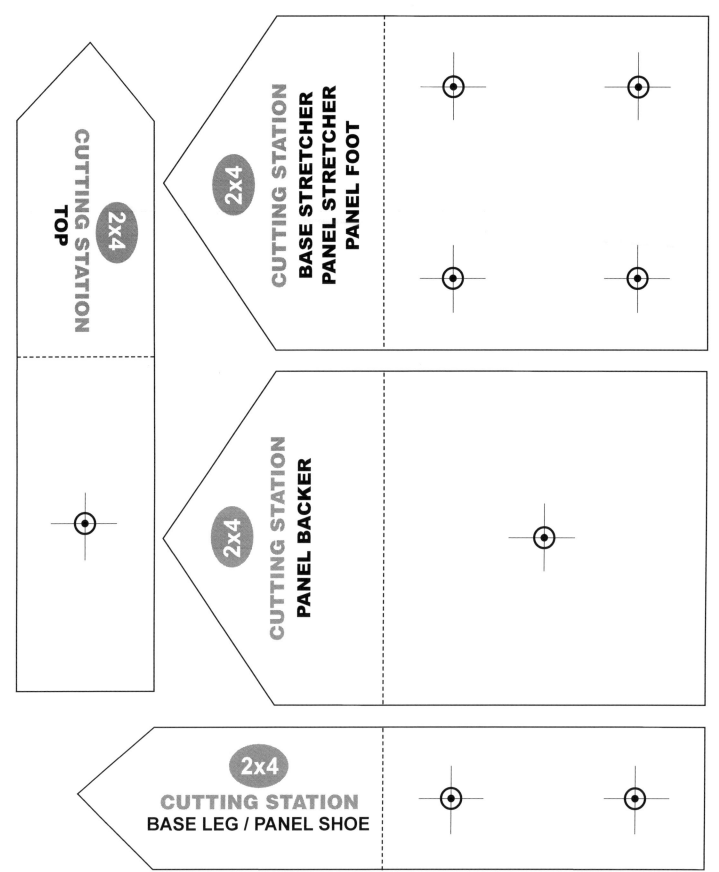

CUTTING STATION
TOP
2x4

CUTTING STATION
BASE STRETCHER
PANEL STRETCHER
PANEL FOOT
2x4

CUTTING STATION
PANEL BACKER
2x4

2x4
CUTTING STATION
BASE LEG / PANEL SHOE

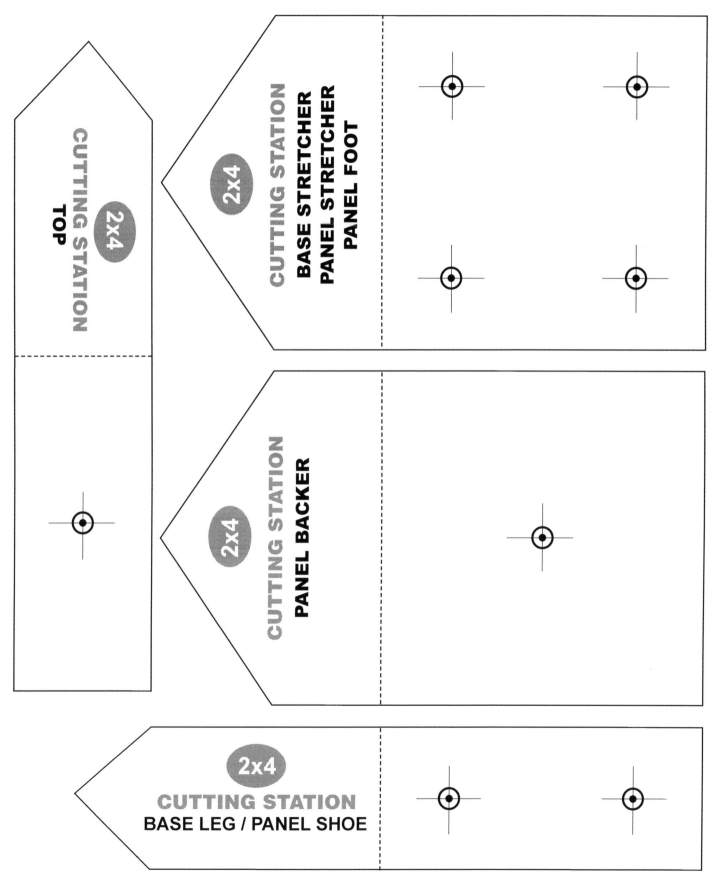

CUTTING STATION
TOP
2x4

2x4
CUTTING STATION
BASE STRETCHER
PANEL STRETCHER
PANEL FOOT

2x4
CUTTING STATION
PANEL BACKER

2x4
CUTTING STATION
BASE LEG / PANEL SHOE

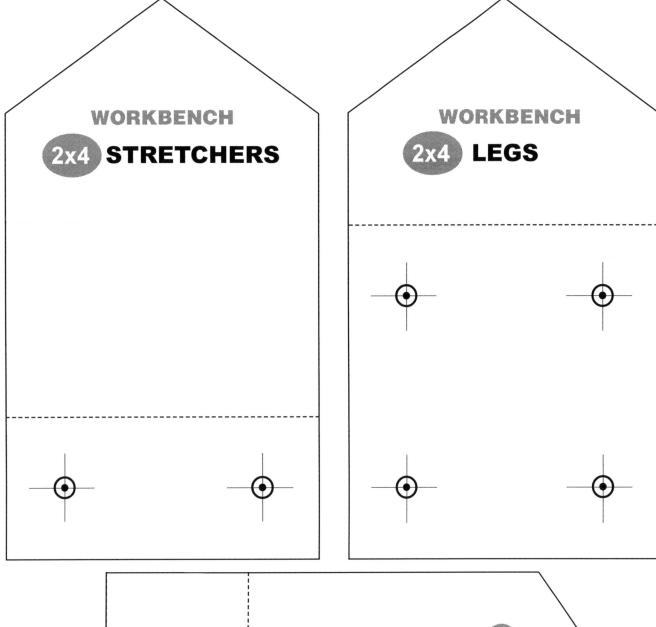

WORKBENCH
2x4 STRETCHERS

WORKBENCH
2x4 LEGS

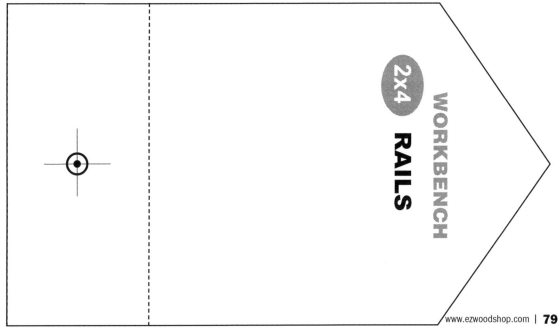

2x4 WORKBENCH RAILS

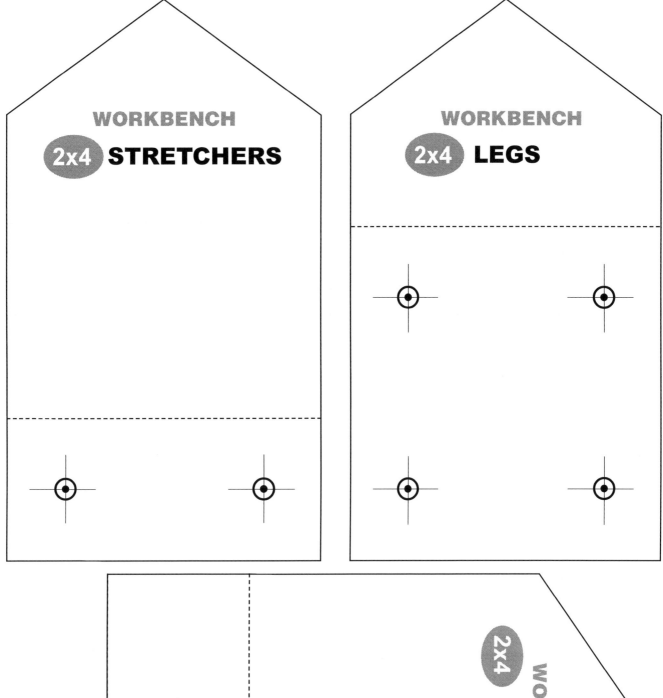

WORKBENCH
2x4 **STRETCHERS**

WORKBENCH
2x4 **LEGS**

2x4 **WORKBENCH RAILS**

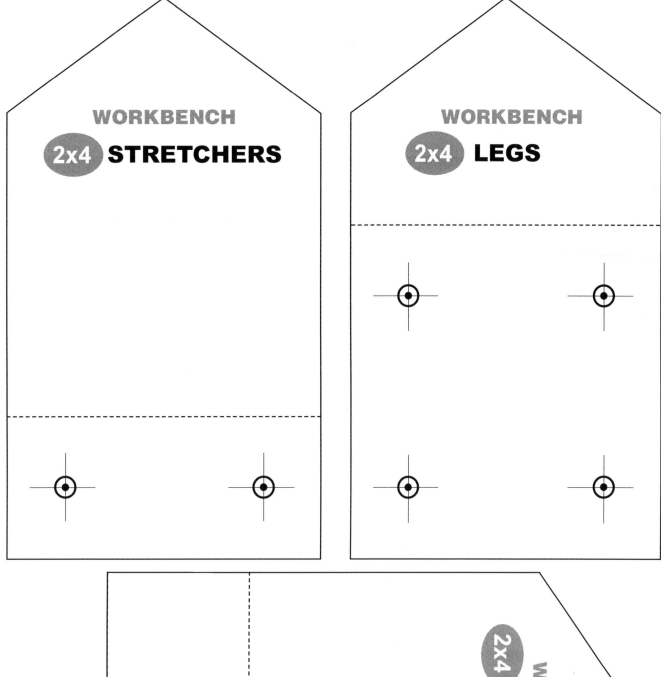

WORKBENCH
2x4 STRETCHERS

WORKBENCH
2x4 LEGS

2x4 WORKBENCH RAILS

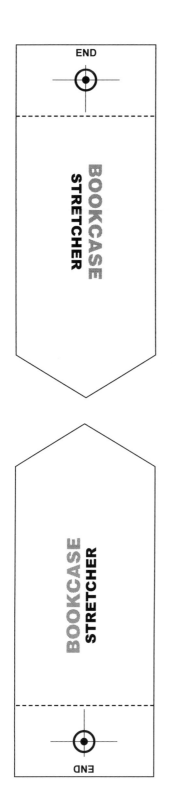

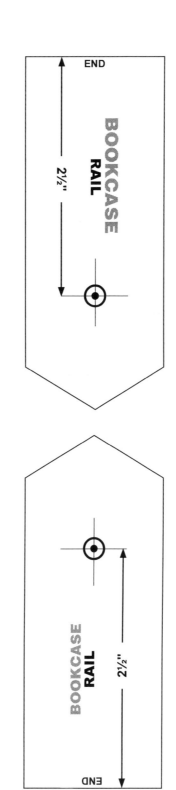

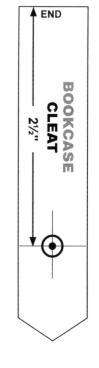

BOOK CUTOUTS

Bookcase
EZ Pilot Hole Guides

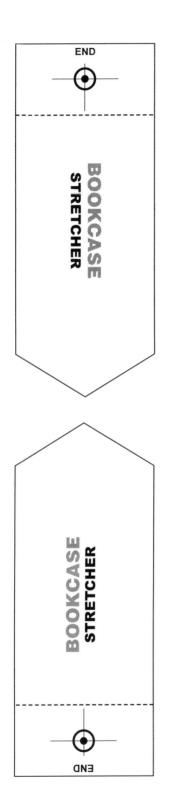

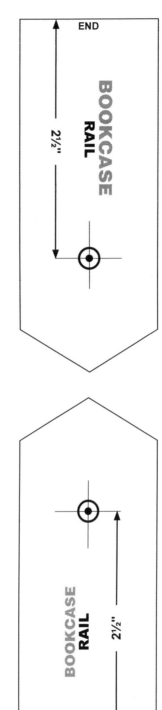

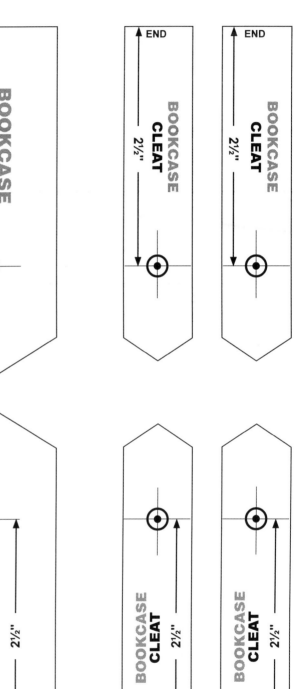

BOOK CUTOUTS

Bookcase
EZ Pilot Hole Guides

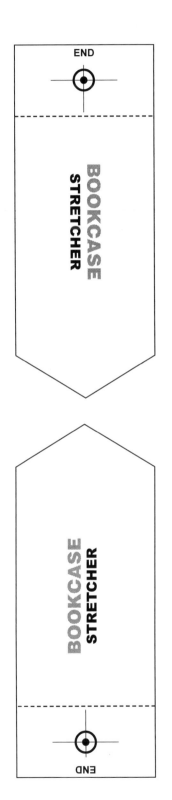

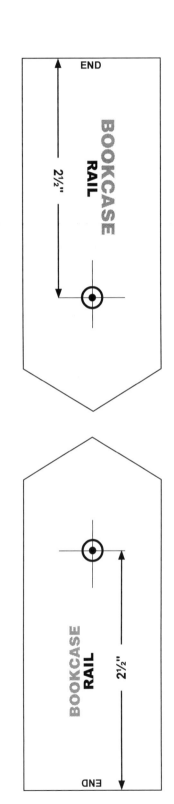

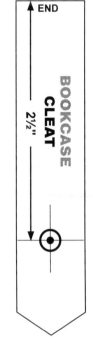

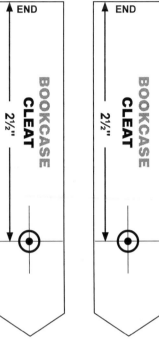